WHAT REVIEWERS SAY ABOUT THIS BOOK:

"While few may have the chance to live with llamas, many can take vicarious pleasure in following the author's experiences, related with warmth and humor... A wealth of practical advice." — American Library Association Booklist

"A look into the warm, touching, friendly, and funny emotions of one couple's developing relationship with llamas. Those who don't have 'llama fever' already can get some insight into what it is like. A must-read for anyone just getting into raising llamas... Both useful and entertaining." — Llamas: The Journal of the Camelid Industry

"Well illustrated, fascinating reading for any animal lover." — The Brayer: Voice of the Donkey and Mule World

AND READERS SAY:

"I cried, I laughed, I learned, and now I'm sold on llamas."

"Received your book soon after we purchased our first llamas. There was a lot of useful information in it for first-time owners. We really enjoyed both the story and the manual side of the book."

"Living with Llamas covers every aspect of llama life... A must for all prospective llama owners or llama lovers!"

"Very entertaining as well as an invaluable learning experience."

"Received the book Friday afternooon, stayed up til 12:30 AM to finish it on Saturday morning. What more can I say?"

Living with Llamas

Adventures, Photos, and a Practical Guide

Rosana Hart

*To Marion –
with best wishes,
Rosana Hart*

Juniper Ridge Press
Ashland, Oregon

TO LLAMAS
and the people who love them

PUBLISHED BY:
Juniper Ridge Press
P O Box 777
Ashland, OR 97520.
Printed in the United States of America.
Back cover: Medford Mail Tribune photo by Steve Johnson.

Second printing, Nov 1985

Library of Congress Cataloging in Publication Data

Hart, Rosana, 1942–
    Living with llamas.

    Bibliography: p.
    Includes index.
    Summary: A personal narrative about life as an owner and breeder of llamas, including a practical section describing the buying, feeding, care, training, and financial aspects of raising llamas.
        1. Llamas as pets.   [1. Llamas as pets]   I. Title.
SF459.L52H37   1985   636.2'96   84-20171
ISBN 0-916289-00-1

Acknowledgements

My thanks begin with the llamas, for being what they are. I especially want to thank Tumbleweed for his encouragement.

I have been helped greatly by those who have written about llamas, and I'd like to thank here all of the writers whose works are listed in the Resource Guide. Particular thanks and appreciation go to Andy Tillman and to Cheryl and Bob Dal Porto.

Bob and Cheryl Dal Porto, Bill Franklin, Bobra Goldsmith, Eric Hoffman, Lake and Lawrence Hunter, Susan L. Jones, Tom and Toni Landis, Dan Schoenthal, Sally and Paul Taylor, Andy Tillman, and Beula and Jim Williams are among the many llama breeders who have shared their knowledge with me. Everyone named read part or all of the manuscript for this book, and made helpful suggestions. Thanks also to Dick and Kay Patterson for their work in breeding and popularizing llamas.

Dori Appel, Betty Huck, Joe Kogel, Lorin Leith, John Machin, and other writers have nudged me to revise and revise again. Many thanks to Arnold Patent, for encouraging me to follow my dreams, and to Dan Poynter, Paul De Fremery, and Michael Bass for helping me turn a dream into a book.

And most of all, thanks to my husband Kelly, for being himself.

About the Author

Rosana Hart is a llama breeder with writing in her blood. With a mother who wrote engineering textbooks for the U.S. Navy and a science-fiction writer father (Cordwainer Smith), Rosana has been writing all her life. She graduated Phi Beta Kappa from Stanford University with a B.A. in Anthropology, and continued her studies in that field as a Woodrow Wilson Fellow at the University of California at Berkeley. She left academia to become a probation officer in Oakland, California, and to travel in Europe. After returning to U.C. Berkeley for a Master's in Library Science, she worked off and on for twelve years as a children's and reference librarian for Sonoma County Library in California. During that time she married filmmaker Kelly Hart and became a stepmother, traveled in Mexico and Guatemala, and studied hypnotherapy under Freda Morris of Hypnosis Clearing House.

She and Kelly moved to Oregon in 1981, and soon after began their llama herd. Rosana has taught self-hypnosis, time management, and related topics through Continuing Education of Southern Oregon State College in Ashland, Oregon, and through Hartworks, a business primarily devoted to Kelly's films. During the warmer months, the Harts take people for short llama walks on their ranch near Ashland, Oregon.

This is her first book. She has plans for more.

Table of Contents

Part I

Our Life with Llamas

1

Before They Came

"Levi is running by the fence," Sally Taylor said. "He has a large spot on his leg--that's how you can tell him from Balzac." Both young llamas were creamy white with dark spots, like chocolate chip ice cream. I found it hard to believe that they were only two weeks old. Their ears moved in the direction of any sound, and their faces already seemed to express ancient wisdom. Balzac looked at us from beside his mother.

Kelly and I were at Riverhole Llamasary to choose our first llama. We watched Levi nurse from a black llama with a white neck.

"That's Fancy, his mother," Sally said. "His father, Rama, is away right now, being used for breeding. Like Levi, he's appaloosa. We think Fancy and Rama are outstanding in looks and intelligence. We gave Levi his name because he has such good genes."

Kelly preferred Levi's pattern of spots, and I liked his name. Spots and a name were funny reasons to select a llama, but Sally knew far more about llamas than we did, and we trusted her evaluation that either young llama would suit our needs. We chose Levi.

Sally loved her animals, I could tell from the gentleness with which she handled them. She and her husband Paul had begun with two llamas a few years ago, and now had over thirty. "I come out and watch them whenever I can," she said. "Sometimes I'm out here for hours. They're such social animals, there's always something going on. Look in the field by the barn."

A dozen llamas were clustered together. "There's a week-old llama in the middle of the herd," Sally said. "We just put her and her mother in with the main herd, and the other females are curious." I could scarcely see the baby, as the llamas were all trying to sniff her. My eyes returned to Levi.

"I'm sure you'll enjoy Levi," Sally said. "What made you decide to get a llama?"

"It just seemed to happen," Kelly replied. "Before we moved to Oregon, I picked up a brochure about going packing with a group called Shasta Llamas. Rosana was working in the library in Santa Rosa then, and she came across a book called Along Came a Llama. We both read it, and were impressed with the intelligence and sensitivity of the llamas."

Next we went to see some llamas, just for curiosity, a pleasant outing for an afternoon. We realized that a llama could be useful to us, for packing and for wool. Sally knew the rest of the story. A few months earlier we put our names on her waiting list for a young male.

"That's how we became interested," I said, "but I'm still puzzling over why."

My background had very few animals in it. I had grown up in an academic family, with my nose in a book. The book might be an animal story, but throughout my childhood I walked several blocks out of my way to avoid large dogs. I studied anthropology in college, became a probation officer and later a librarian, taught self-hypnosis and time management, and travelled around the world. Only occasionally would a dog scare me any more.

Kelly had at least grown up in a rural area. There were sometimes sheep or cattle on the land his parents owned, and he helped with the animals. He had grown up to become a film animator, jazz saxophone player, and carpenter. He loved plants, animals, and inspiring views.

In our life together we evolved a style which was in some ways close to the land, and in other ways rushed and urban. We kept chickens and vegetable gardens. We lived by the ocean and in an old summer camp set in apple orchards. While I worked in a busy public library system, Kelly made films and obtained a patent on a method of animation.

We had just moved to seventy undeveloped acres in the rugged mountains of southern Oregon. We were living in a trailer and putting in water, electricity, and a garden.

The land was steep and dry, reminding Kelly of southern Idaho where he had grown up.   The urban amenities we craved were just twenty minutes away, in Ashland, a town which combined the friendliness of rural Oregon with the sophistication of being a world-renowned theatrical center.   It would be a good time to bring a llama into our lives.

We would have to wait six months for Levi to grow up and be weaned from his mother before he could come to us.   As we left Riverhole Llamasary, I felt the same excitement mixed with unreality I had felt when we bought our land.   Dreams coming true generally led to surprises--usually pleasant--and more dreams.   Levi would be our llama, and I wondered what it would really be like.   Maybe someday we would have a whole herd of llamas.

Sally sent us photos of Levi--he gazed at us from the refrigerator door, along with a Peruvian postcard of a llama herd I found in the house where I grew up.   My father or grandfather must have picked it up in their travels, some time in the past fifty years, little imagining that llamas would become a topic of intense interest to their descendent.   I was sorry they had both died before I could ask them about it.

Sally wrote that Levi was more oriented toward people than most of the other baby llamas.   That seemed good, since we were only going to have one llama.   We knew that llamas were likely to be lonely if kept by themselves.   Many breeders would only sell them in pairs.

Our plan was for Levi to become friends with our dogs.   I talked with a man who had one llama and took it jogging with him frequently.   It lived in a back yard with a puppy, received lots of human attention, and so far as anyone could tell, was perfectly happy.

I thought our dogs would probably get along well with Levi.   Martha, now thirteen, was happy to spend long hours under the kitchen table, becoming lively only when food appeared.   I didn't expect her to pay much attention to llamas.

Cider would.   A puppy just a few weeks older than Levi, she was growing into a long-legged, large dog, loving to run.   A Rhodesian Ridgeback, she was of a

Llamas near Cuzco, Peru, some time in the last half-century.
(Peruvian postcard)

breed developed in Africa to hunt lions. Sometimes Martha let Cider attack her, but we were Cider's main playmates. I was looking forward to the llama's help in entertaining Cider and hoping that the entertainment would be mutual.

The months passed, a waiting time. It was a little like being pregnant, but Levi had already been born. We read whatever we could find about llamas, and learned more of their history.

The llama is a South American animal, part of the camel family. Like camels, they have padded, even-toed feet and split lips. I was surprised to learn that their common ancestors originated in North America and lived on this continent for over forty million years. They evolved into camels in Asia and Africa and the lama family (llamas, alpacas, vicunas, and guanacos) in South America. They had only been gone from this continent some ten or twelve thousand years.

In South America, the lamas live mainly in the high Andes. Vicunas and guanacos are wild animals. Vicunas are famed for their fine wool; its softness has brought them to the brink of extinction. Guanacos may be the forerunners of llamas; the two species are similar in many respects, though the guanaco's wool is fine and shorter, and with a greater commercial value in South America. While guanacos do not have the official status of endangered, their numbers are a tiny fraction of what they were a century ago.

Alpacas and llamas have been domesticated for centuries. Alpaca wool has also been more highly prized than that of the llama. There are relatively few alpacas in North America. Archaeological findings indicate that

Camels are close relatives of llamas. This one, at the Patterson Ranch, Sisters, Oregon has returned to the continent of its earliest ancestors.

Llamas in the treeless Bolivian highlands; they are not wild, but are allowed to graze freely. (Wilhelmine Afra Chance)

llamas were living with man by 3000 B.C. The vast Inca empire, which reached its peak toward the end of the Middle Ages in Europe, used llamas in many ways. They were beasts of burden, essential in a mountainous society that had not invented the wheel. Their wool was used for blankets, ponchos, and other items. They played an important part in the religious and ceremonial life of the Incas: many llamas were sacrificed to the gods.

Probably the world's most versatile domestic animal, llamas are still used as beasts of burden and for wool, primarily in the Bolivian and Peruvian highlands. Their dung is used for fuel--it is said to be odorless when burned. Less and less are llamas used for long-distance transport, though, as trucks reach further into remote areas.

Llamas were brought to the United States during the nineteenth century and early in this one, by William Randolph Hearst and others. In the 1930s, an importation ban was imposed on South American livestock, for fear that they might bring in foot and mouth disease. The ban was recently lifted for Chile, and some llamas, alpacas, and llama-alpaca crosses were brought into the United States. Then the ban was reinstated, and it is not yet clear whether further importation will be permitted.

There are approximately eight thousand llamas in this country now. They have become more popular in the past decade, and are being used more and more for backpacking. Organizations devoted to llamas have been started.

One organization, the International Llama Association, was sponsoring a conference in Sunriver, a resort in eastern Oregon. I had been looking forward to it, but

For centuries, llamas have been a motif in South American folk art. Here, Indians and llamas stroll in a Peruvian village. (From a contemporary Peruvian painting on glass)

when Kelly and I walked into the large wood-beamed
conference hall filled with hundreds of chatting llama
owners, I felt intimidated.

"Kelly! Rosana! What are you doing here? Do you
have llamas?" We turned to see an old friend, Tanya
Charter, whom we hadn't seen in several years. During
that time she had acquired some llamas. She introduced
us to a couple sitting with her, and they turned out to
know one of Kelly's sisters. Small world. I stopped
feeling shy, and delved into three intense days of
information about breeding, training demonstrations, and
discussions of how to comb or shear them.

"Do you pronounce llama 'lama' or 'yama'?" I asked
llama owners. Though 'yama' was the Indian and Spanish
pronunciation, most called their animals 'lamas.' So we did
too.

One evening at the exhibit booths, I bought a copy of
Speechless Brothers, by Andy Tillman, a history of llamas
and comprehensive guide to llama care. At bedtime I
thought I would glance through a few pages. It was after
three in the morning when I finally turned out the light,
and my dreams were filled with llamas, South American
Indians, and mountain trails.

The conference wound up with a tour of the ranch of
Dick and Kay Patterson in Sisters, Oregon, containing the
largest herd of llamas in the United States. It was
astonishing to see over five hundred llamas in one place.
The llamas came running to see the hundreds of humans
too.

The late afternoon sun blinked through miles of pine
forests as we drove home, thinking it all over. When I

Tanya's llamas have a hard life. (Drawing by David Moore)

asked, "What makes a beautiful llama?" people answered in many different ways. There were no official or written standards. I liked Dick Patterson's rejoinder, "What's a beautiful woman, a beautiful horse, a beautiful painting? It's in the eye of the beholder."

I felt enthusiastic about llamas, and I talked to Kelly about maybe becoming breeders ourselves. If what we had heard at the conference was correct, llamas were an excellent investment. I thought we could make part of our living by raising them. It would be a lot of fun.

Kelly was driving. He didn't seem to be as involved in my daydreams as I was. He knew I tended to get carried away. Then he said, "What about small llamas?"

"Huh?"

"I wonder if we could breed small llamas," he said. "Most people seem to favor the large animals, and that makes sense for wilderness packing. But what about people who might just want one or two llamas for pets? Small ones would still be useful for backpacking, even though they would carry less. They could travel in smaller vehicles, too."

"Small ones would be good for people like me, who are intimidated by large animals," I reflected. "That one time I was on a horse has left its mark on me." At an uncle's ranch one summer, I had gone for a long ride on a horse who tried to scrape me off into the trees. I was still afraid of riding.

Another reason for small llamas occurred to me. "Weavers might be interested. What if a smaller llama with long wool could produce roughly the same amount of wool as larger llamas with shorter wool? It could be like dwarf fruit trees."

"I don't know if it would be hard to breed them, but it would be fun to try," Kelly said. "I've been thinking about Tumbleweed. Remember him?"

Indeed I did. He was an exceptionally small young male llama at Riverhole Llamasary. Tumbleweed had a dear face, with a bit of hay usually dangling Huck Finn-style from his mouth. His wool was longer than Levi's. Like Levi, he had appaloosa markings.

I remembered that Sally thought he was special too. "Would they sell him? How could we know if he carries genes for smallness? Maybe he's just stunted in his growth for some reason."

"His mother was on the small side, and Sally mentioned a small half-brother from the same father," Kelly remembered.

"Sounds good."

"Seems like we're getting serious here," Kelly said. "When I pick up Ajila and Levi, shall I try to buy Tumbleweed?" He would soon be going to the San Francisco airport to meet his daughter's flight from New Orleans. On the way home, they would pick up Levi.

"Sure! I guess you can fit Ajila and her luggage and two llamas into the van. I wonder what she'll think of all this. So we don't have any llamas yet, but we have an official breeding plan, small llamas with long wool. I wonder if we could breed for good disposition too. Llamas generally seem to be good natured, but there's bound to be some variation."

"I don't know how much that's a matter of inheritance," said Kelly, "but let's go for it."

2

First Days

Kelly, his daughter Ajila, and two young llamas drove north through the hot central valley of California. Kelly had made this trip many times before, but this time it was different. Here he was with the daughter he hadn't seen for a year, and they were sharing the van with two strange animals. How do you communicate with a daughter turned teenager? With llamas?

At first Levi and Tumbleweed stood up, but as they became accustomed to the rolling motion of the vehicle, they sat down between the built-in bed and the sink. The window shades in back were pulled down so the llamas wouldn't be distracted by things outside the window. Neither had ever traveled before.

Ajila went back and scratched their necks. Levi stretched his neck toward her as she rubbed.

The llamas were making humming sounds with an inquisitive tone. It was easy to translate those to something like, "What's going on here?" It was harder to interpret the hums that were more of a monotone. Kelly knew that llamas are social animals who use sounds and body language to communicate. Understanding them was going to be like learning a new language. Ajila imitated the sounds.

In the hazy heat, a traffic tie-up forced them to stop. Cars and trucks were parked as far ahead as they could see. The llamas stood up and began exploring their surroundings, pulling at the velcro on the curtains and sniffing Ajila's guitar case. Kelly talked to the other motorists. There was a chemical spill a few miles north of them, and the freeway had already been closed for twenty-four hours. A trucker said that the road was expected to be open again in two more hours.

Kelly pulled the van into the shade of a large truck, and they waited. Ajila pulled out some playing cards, and she and Kelly played desultory hands of gin rummy.

Tumbleweed was foaming at the mouth. Was it from the worming medicine Sally had given him by mouth that morning? Kelly hoped so. He thought so. But still he felt like a new father, not sure what to do.

He pulled up handfuls of tall grass--not yet dried by the summer sun--from the roadside. Ajila offered it to the llamas, who seemed happy to munch. Tumbleweed's foam disappeared, and Kelly's anxiety along with it. He and Ajila continued to pick grass. What else to do, anyway?

The llamas ate, and soon Levi followed a natural inclination. Luckily, llamas' droppings are much like deer's, little pellets, easy to clean up. Tumbleweed sniffed where Levi had gone, and he followed suit. Kelly grabbed a shoe box and tried to catch the cascade of pellets. At that moment, car engines around them started up. Kelly threw the shoe box down, Ajila jumped in the van, and they began moving north again.

At home, I was looking down our long dirt driveway every few minutes. Would there be one llama, or two? How would Ajila have changed? She had spent most summers with us since she was two. I loved the first look at her, seeing what letters, phone calls, and even snapshots couldn't convey. The combination of her and Levi--and maybe Tumbleweed--had me scatter-brained with anticipation.

When the van finally came up our driveway, Kelly grinned and held up two fingers. Then I saw the two woolly heads.

After hugs and hellos, we coaxed our new llamas out of the van by tugging on the lead ropes attached to their halters. The light breeze lifted their fuzzy wool, and the late afternoon sun made shadow patterns on it. The llamas looked around.

Our dogs investigated the newcomers. Cider, the puppy, jumped on Ajila and ran long-legged circles around the llamas, inviting them to play. They watched her. Martha, the ancient one, surprised me by barking and trying to nip at the llamas' back feet. They watched her too, and deftly stepped out of her way.

Ajila was exploring. We had moved since her last visit, and it was all new to her. "Wow, what a view!" she said, looking south to where snow-covered Mount Shasta, some fifty miles away, was gleaming.

"Which is your land?" she asked.

"Let's walk up to the ridge with the llamas—we can show you better from there."

Kelly and I were each holding one llama's lead rope. I was holding on tightly, watching whatever Levi did. Both llamas walked easily on lead, sniffing at each other and us, leaning over for a mouthful of one plant or another. The dogs came along, Martha growling intermittently at the llamas.

"Kelly, the llamas are really here! Both of them!"

"Yes, I got excited when Sally said she'd sell Tumbleweed too. Hey, they're pointing their ears forward, maybe because of the squirrel under the juniper tree. They sure do watch things."

Levi sniffed my shoulder. Tumbleweed stayed further away from us. He seemed to be more adventurous about exploring new places, as he went along the ridge from one snack to another. Kelly followed at the other end of the rope. The two llamas were already showing differences; I wondered how distinct their personalities would be. I liked how they both blended calmness and curiosity.

Kelly showed Ajila the boundaries of our land. From the ridge, the cliffs dropped down to a flat meadow. "We like to hike below the cliffs," he told Ajila. "We have sixteen acres down there, including a place we call the magic place. We'll take you there. We're planning to live on top here—we'll build an addition to the trailer. There will be llama sheds beyond it, and eventually I want a studio up near the ridge."

Ajila looked at the 360 degree view of mountains, turning luminous as the sun set. "Sure is different from Louisiana," she said.

As the evening progressed, I kept popping out to the llama yard, to watch how the llamas sat down, or stood up, or had a drink of water. Once Levi rolled over on his back—to scratch it, I surmised. The llama yard had been the dog yard; now the dogs were in the trailer,

where they much preferred to be, and the llamas had a
space the size of a small suburban back yard, sloping up
the hill by the trailer. A large juniper tree provided
shade and nibbles. A few bushes provided more nibbles,
and there was some grass.

The main course was alfalfa hay, in and around a
cardboard box. I had brought the hay home in our tiny
station wagon, carefully arranging it so I could fit three
bales in. Munching hay, the llamas seemed right at
home.

Ajila considered her choice of accommodations. The
tiny second bedroom in the trailer was already my study,
so we offered her our camping tent, pitched on a flat
place next to the llama yard, or the van, which still
smelled from the journey. She chose the tent, and neatly
arranged her things in it. Cider slept with her in the
tent, an arrangement which didn't last past the second
chewing of our good down comforter.

Kelly and I walked up to the ridge. There was a
breeze, as usual; our land was in a mountain pass, so if
the wind wasn't blowing from California, it was probably
blowing from Oregon. This evening it was blowing from
the south, appropriately, I thought, considering how much
had just blown in from California.

The western sky was still glowing as we strolled hand
in hand. As we came back toward the trailer, the llamas
were sitting with their legs tucked under them. Levi's
ears were forward, Tumbleweed's were back.

"I thought ears back was an aggressive signal," Kelly
commented, "but I think Tumbleweed just keeps his that
way. While I was driving, I watched the llamas in the
rear-view mirror, and his ears were back most of the
time."

"He hardly looks aggressive now," I said. "Hi,
Tumbleweed, I'm so glad you're here." Tumbleweed and
Levi were gently chewing.

We could see them from our bedroom window. I woke
up several times during the night, and looked out, but
there was no moon and nothing much was visible. At
first light I woke again, and peered out. Levi was sitting
tucked up, and he was looking at me. I was thrilled. He
continued chewing his cud.

We were living with llamas now, and our attention was

riveted on these fascinating additions to our family. Excitement alternated with wondering what we'd gotten into; what commitment not yet fully understood had been made? It was, of course, much less of a commitment than being new parents; we could always sell the llamas.

But it was the same kind of uncertainty. What did we need to do for them? What should we allow them to do, and how to train them to do what we wanted and not what we didn't want?

One afternoon, I watched them chase each other around the yard, biting knees and necks and ears. I worried that they would hurt each other, and ran to phone another llama breeder. "It's good exercise," he assured me. "They won't grow fighting teeth for another year or two. Don't worry." Fighting teeth were very sharp, and were removed by llama owners who kept males in the same pasture.

We put Cider in the corral with the llamas; after all, it was the dog yard. She would whine and bark to get out, but the llamas didn't seem to notice. She ate their hay with them. Tumbleweed sniffed her cautiously, backing off if she moved quickly. Sometimes she ran around them, play-attacking, showing her hunting-dog ancestry. After Levi gave her a kick, she was less rambunctious with him.

We staked the llamas out to graze among the rabbit brush and other high-desert types of vegetation on our land. By staking Levi and Tumbleweed at different places around the land, we could provide them with munchies and diversion, and they could be our roving lawn mowers. We attached them by twenty-foot ropes to cinder blocks or to trees. I wondered if they would nibble on their ropes, as Cider did on her leash; they didn't. We stopped using cinder blocks, though, after Levi dragged one a fourth of mile, to where Tumbleweed and I were walking.

Whenever we staked them near our half-completed septic tank installation, a llama or two climbed the mound of dirt beside the tank. They would stand there, gazing majestically at everything around them: passing cars, forests, mountains, clouds. Alert to sound and movement, they stood.

Now and then one would tangle a rope around a tree

Kelly's sister Molly observes Levi, who is more interested in the camera. (Rebecca Hart)

or some bushes; or if we let them graze close together, they would intertwine their ropes. Then they would just sit down, and soon one of us would notice and straighten them out.

We checked on them frequently, leaving our gardening or ranch work, or running outside if we were in the trailer. They didn't need checking---tangled lines were rare--but we had become as curious as llamas. I would be writing, or planning a class, when I would have to find out what they were doing. I felt as though beings as magical as elves or unicorns had come to live with us. What did they think about? What is thinking for a llama? What kinds of emotions did they feel? Did they have a sense of humor? I wondered and watched.

"It's the Lee and Tee Show," joked Kelly as he came upon me gazing at the llamas. Lee and Tee stuck as nicknames.

Kelly was reading in the trailer one afternoon, when he looked up and saw Levi walking past. Levi was wandering slowly up toward the ridge, nibbling here and there. Kelly followed in what he hoped was a casual manner. Levi seemed to be enjoying his freedom, and aware that something was different. He leaned over to nibble, and Kelly grabbed him by the neck. Levi didn't seem to mind. It wasn't to be our last loose llama.

Late in the summer, Kelly's three sisters came to visit, bringing most of their children. Our eight-year-old nephew Reb spent hours catching Tumbleweed and walking him around. Reb would let Tumbleweed go, only to catch him again five minutes later. Tumble became much easier to catch, and after Reb's visit he seemed to prefer children to adults.

One sultry afternoon we all went on a long hike. Our destination was the "magic place" below our cliffs. Kelly

Tumbleweed and our nephew Reb are good friends. (Rebecca Hart)

set off first, with Lee and Tee and some of the crowd. I filled up the car with everybody else, to meet the hikers where our route would leave the paved road.

As I drove around a bend in the road, there they were: half-a-dozen people in colorful summer shorts and tops. Our bright blue day-pack identified Kelly. The llamas were in the midst of the group. They were a charming sight, and it was fun for me to come upon them, since I was usually with the llamas.

We parked, and waited for the others to catch up with us. "Rosana, can Levi count?" asked eleven-year-old Soral.

"I don't think so," I answered. "Why? Did you see him counting something?"

"No, but when we went for a walk with him yesterday, I was way behind everybody, picking flowers. I went into the bushes to pick some more flowers, and nobody could see me. Levi stopped and wouldn't go till I came back and he saw me. So I thought maybe he was counting everybody."

"I don't think he was counting," I answered. "Maybe it was just a coincidence that he stopped right then. Levi can be balky sometimes."

Kelly's sister Alexandra was leading Levi, and she gave Soral his lead rope. We all hiked together, everyone taking turns with the llamas. Kelly and I didn't let the llamas nibble while hiking, as it slowed things down too much, but the others were more casual. The llamas were good judges of what they could get away with, and this time they got away with a lot.

We passed a cow pie in the road. Levi leaned over and sniffed it. He must have taken a small nibble, as he made faces.

We arrived at the magic place. A large pyramid-shaped boulder marked the entrance to a grove of maple trees. We tied the llamas to a tree, where they could nibble on the leaves, and we showed off this favorite area of ours. Boulders had fallen off the cliffs over the centuries, and maples had grown tall around them. It was cool and mossy under the trees, with maple leaves blown into soft beds here and there. The entrances to homes of tiny animals were visible between groupings of rocks.

Kelly first found this place when he was hiking alone. It began to rain, and he took refuge in a space under two boulders. There was even a ledge to sit on. It had the feeling of Mayan temples we had visited in southern Mexico and Guatemala.

Everyone explored for a while, and we spread out a picnic. It was dusk when we untied the llamas and slowly made our way back up the trail. When we reached the car, I had more volunteers for a ride. The hiking group continued ahead while we filled up the car.

When we drove past Kelly and Levi, Kelly called out for us to stop. "Levi keeps turning around and looking for you behind us," he said. "Better let him see that it's you in the car."

I thought, "So Soral was right. Levi does keep track." Once Levi had seen us, he followed Kelly home with no further fuss.

3

Posey

After owning Levi and Tumbleweed for several weeks, we knew we wanted to become llama breeders. Our fascination with the animals, and our respect for them, was increasing as we learned more about our two. We were spending a lot of time with them, but their essential care didn't take long.

Breeding would be an enjoyable way to earn part of our living. We had the money to buy a female or two, and investing in llamas seemed a totally positive act. From what we had seen so far, llamas were good for people, bringing out a sense of wonder and delight.

I was concerned about my ability to become a llama midwife. Llama births were usually normal, but now and then human help would be needed. What if I were home alone and had to help a llama give birth?

While we were thinking about it, I received a phone call from a llama owner who lived nearby. Their first llama birth had been the day before, and Lizabee was bubbling with enthusiasm. She came home from shopping to find four llamas in a field where there had been three.

It seemed that the new little llama had been born just a few minutes earlier. He wasn't nursing yet. She decided to milk the mother, just to make sure all the teats were unclogged. "I've never milked an animal in my life, but when you have to, you learn!" she said.

He began nursing soon, but over the next few hours he became weaker. "So I gave him an enema--and believe me, I'd never given an animal an enema either. But I did it, and almost as soon as I finished, he perked right up."

I was impressed. "How did you know what to do?"

"I just knew what I'd heard at the conference, and what I'd read. Luckily, I knew what I needed to know. It sure was thrilling."

The first night she slept out in the llama pasture, taking along household dogs and cats for company, waking up frequently to look at the new baby lying by its mother, both clearly outlined in the moonlight.

If she could learn, I could learn. Kelly and I went to take a look at two female llamas we had heard about at the llama conference. We didn't like the looks of the first llama. We learned from her that we were beginning to develop our taste in llama conformation.

We had heard a lot about the second female at the llama conference. The man selling her, Dan Schoenthal, had been very helpful, full of advice and opinions on all aspects of llama care. He was especially fond of this female, as she was the first llama he had seen being born. "Posey is practically Dan's daughter," a friend had joked.

We knew that Posey was about a year old. She had long brown wool, a white neck, and some black on her face. At the conference we had peered at slides held up to the light, but we hadn't been able to tell much.

She was being kept at Tom and Toni Landis' place. We arrived around noon on a hot summer day. Situated in rolling hills, it had both a nice view and privacy. Llamas were grazing in the pastures and standing under several deep shade trees. Tom came out to greet us. "Glad to see you found the place," he said. "I bet you'd like to see Posey first thing."

She stood in the field among the other llamas. She was slight of frame, not very short but delicate. She was totally feminine. Her eyes were large and brown, complete with long, long lashes. There was something coquettish about her walk as she approached the fence, cautiously coming closer for a better look at us.

Toni had told me at the conference, "We named her Posey because she reminded us of a ladylike young ballerina, one still in the chorus." It was an apt description here, with the other llamas moving gracefully behind her. There was one other llama watching us, a young black one. She moved away, and my attention

Posey. (Medford Mail Tribune photo by Steve Johnson)

returned to Posey.

Tom brought a rope, and we caught her after a little chase. Once caught, she submitted--with a slight tremble--to being handled. She came up right next to me and blew on my face. I blew back; this was a llama greeting I knew. She continued blowing, nuzzling my face, sniffing my ears. I had never been so thoroughly cuddled by a llama. I was enchanted. I thought briefly of the poison oak in the pasture, and decided it was worth some risk for this sensitive touch, this sweet alfalfa breath blowing on my face and hair.

"How friendly you are," I murmured to Posey, my attention riveted to her like a lover's. Posey and I were in our little cocoon world, and I don't know which one of us finally pulled away.

"She's a real sweetheart," Kelly was saying. "Does she come up to everyone like that?"

"No, not at all," Tom replied. "Rosana made a real hit."

"So did she," I said, still in a daze of emotion.

Kelly was holding her lead rope now, feeling her wool and being nuzzled. I tried to come out of my daze. Emotion was no way to buy an expensive animal, I told myself. Think of her conformation, her wool, her genealogy. Ask about any weaknesses or possible problems. So I did all that. Kelly had some questions too. The answers were satisfactory. They had a carefully tended ranch here, we could tell, and it was evident that the animals received good care. Within fifteen minutes Posey was ours. I went inside and had a good wash with some anti-poison oak stuff of Tom's.

We were travelling in our little Subaru station wagon, thinking of this trip as an exploratory expedition. We hadn't planned on coming home with a llama. But Kelly said, "I wonder if Posey might fit in the back of the car." If we packed our overnight bags on top, it seemed there would be room.

There was. Tom found someone else to help, and it took two of us pulling on Posey's lead rope from the front, and two shoving her flailing legs in from the rear. Quickly there was one surprised llama in the back of our small car. She grunted a little as we shoved her in; then she settled down to a steady stream of inquisitive hums

and huhs. As we prepared to leave, I put my face up to
hers. She blew on me. I blew back, and we were off.

It was several hours, mostly on freeways, to our
place. Posey continued her questioning hums; I answered
by telling her about Levi, Tumbleweed, and all the fine
llama babies she would have. Now and then I turned
around, and we rubbed noses.

Posey moved around sideways until she was looking out
the back window. I was surprised that few motorists
noticed.

One car did pull up next to us. "What's that, a
goat?" hollered the driver.

"A LLAMA!" Kelly and I chorused. The fellow
grinned.

We arrived home late in the afternoon. As we took
Posey out of the car, both males were at the edge of
their yard, eagerly watching. Posey saw them right
away, and stood up very tall. Since we hadn't planned to
come home with a llama, we didn't have a second fenced
area. We tied Posey to a tree.

Posey didn't like being tied up. She ran around and
around, lunging to the end of her rope. Llamas learn
very quickly, though, and within five minutes she knew
how far she could run. Then it seemed less that she was
alarmed, and more that she was just frisky. After a
while she settled down.

"We'll take you out to dinner to celebrate your new
llama," offered Jan and Molly, friends who had been
llama-sitting while we were away. I wanted to stay
home with Posey, but everyone else went out to eat.

It was still warm after the hot day. I sat on the
steps of the trailer, watching Posey. What a lovely
creature she was, grazing there, and what a turn our
lives were taking. A year ago we had been waiting for
our home in California to sell, hoping that the third
would-be sale wouldn't fall through as the others had,
hoping that we would be able to buy this land in Oregon.
Now I was not only a country homesteader, but a genuine
llama breeder as well.

Astonishing, wonderful--and also puzzling. Kelly and I
had made a series of decisions over the years, as anyone
does, about where to live, what work to do. Somehow
our decisions had led to this moment. Here I sat,

enjoying the evening, feeling the peacefulness of being a solitary human surrounded by land, trees, and animals. I was a contented little speck in the panorama of mountains, surprised at how naturally my city-bred self had come to love this solitude.

Living with llamas was good for my maternal impulses. I had already noticed how much I enjoyed being a mother hen. Or in this case, mama llama.

My newest charge was grazing a little, watching the other llamas, watching me. A thunderstorm was building, far to the east. As the noise of the thunderbolts increased, Posey began running around again.

I went down by her tree and took her rope in my hand, then very slowly moved toward her. She trembled a little as I approached, but as before, once I was close, she nuzzled me and seemed glad of the comfort. We had a long tete-a-tete, only broken when a loud thunderclap sent her scurrying.

The storm didn't seem to bother Lee or Tee; they were just standing in their yard. After several bright lightning flashes from the eastern horizon, Levi stared steadily in that direction.

I decided to put Posey in the llama yard and stake out the males. She couldn't be in with them because we didn't want her pregnant. It was unlikely that she could be yet, or that these young males could do the job, but we didn't want to risk it.

Levi was easy to catch, but Tumbleweed eluded me. He could run faster than I, and he wasn't in the mood to be caught. I tried maneuvering him between Levi and the fence, a trick which often worked, but Tumble wasn't having any. Frustrated, I gave up until the others returned.

Lee and Tee liked being staked out, so long as they had good grazing around. We kept them staked for three days, while we fenced another area, making sure that somebody was home all that time. Since the llamas wouldn't be able to run away from any dogs that came along, we felt protective. As it happened, an unfamiliar dog did wander in. It was old and gentle, and soon left. The llamas weren't disturbed.

We used six-foot field fencing for the new, larger llama yard, even though many llama owners put up fences of four feet. They probably didn't have four feet of snow or drifts seven feet high. The wire mesh of the fence kept out a porcupine that came by, and we were glad. Our llamas liked to investigate strange new things by putting their noses close and blowing.

Dan phoned the day after we brought Posey home, to hear how she was doing. After I filled him in, I asked him about something Kelly had noticed. Posey seemed nervous around our dogs. The funny thing was that she seemed more upset by lazy old Martha than by wild and crazy Cider.

"She has good reason to be watchful around dogs," said Dan. "When she was just a few months old, some dogs from the neighborhood got into the llama pasture, and chased her and another young one very roughly. They didn't hurt Posey, just scared her--but they injured the other little one so badly that we had to put it down."

"Do you know what the dogs looked like?"

"I didn't see them, but I'd guess from Posey's behavior that they looked something like the dog she's afraid of. She'll settle down, though, don't worry. After that incident, we moved her up to Tom and Toni's place. They have a dog up there, and after Posey had seen it a few times, she was fine with it. I think these dogs of yours are the first ones she's seen since then. She's smart, she'll learn fast that it's okay."

Dan was right; soon Posey became accustomed to our dogs. She reversed her reaction to them, becoming indifferent to Martha but vigilant toward Cider's exuberant movements. She and Cider sometimes sniffed noses through the fence.

As we came to know her, we realized what a very different personality Posey had from the males. Where they were placid, she was temperamental. Where Levi would walk right up to anything he wanted to investigate, Posey would go back and forth. Where Tumbleweed was aloof until caught, she was flighty. Where the males were companionable when on lead, she was affectionate.

Posey and the male llamas spent hours staring at each other across the fences. We wondered if she was lonely, but loneliness wasn't really the issue in the way she watched Levi and Tumbleweed. It was the great drama of being male and female.

The first morning that Posey was here, Kelly took Levi, on lead, up to her fence. The two llamas sniffed noses through the fence, and then Posey made a loud snorting sound she had been making at the males. She raised herself up very tall. Levi put his neck down low, and flipped his tail onto his back, indicating submission. We imagined that Posey was saying, "I'm hot stuff! Better watch out if you're gonna mess with me!" and Levi was responding, "It's cool, babe."

When we took Tumbleweed over, he and Posey went through the same routine. Kelly took Tumble into Posey's yard, still on lead. After a while they quit the display, and stood around near each other, doing nothing in particular.

Tumbleweed's lowered head and neck, and flipped-up tail, indicate submission. We call this the 'low-rider' position, and both young males often used it with Posey.

Male llamas are used for packing, but the females are generally kept home to have the best conditions for pregnancy. Once females reach adulthood, they're pregnant most of the time: a female carries her young for about eleven and a half months, and can usually be bred again two weeks after delivery.

Posey was too young for such things, and we enjoyed taking her on walks. She liked to nibble. Her favorite stop was at a small maple tree on an old dirt road we called Llama Lane. If she failed to munch a few maple leaves on the outward journey, she never missed them on the way home.

When I wore a bright orange tee-shirt with a large appliqued flower, Posey leaned over and sniffed the flower several times as we strolled.

We took her out for walks with one or both of the males. They would do their usual courtship activities, the males walking along with low necks and flipped-over tails, Posey walking with her back legs wider apart. We called it "junior high dance time."

Kids who camped out in the tent next to Posey's yard discovered that when they played loud rock music, Posey came over to the fence and peered in at them. If someone approached the fence quickly, Posey would run away quickly; she seemed always poised to retreat. But if they approached slowly, she might favor them with soft blowings of her alfalfa-scented breath.

Posey was fond of one of our guests, a man with dark hair and a dark beard. She would approach him surely, linger next to him. We wondered what his charm was--and then remembered that Dan, Posey's former owner, had brown hair and a dark beard.

That made us realize just how much llamas can tell different people apart. We had noticed that if we walked up to the fence with a guest, any of the llamas would pay more attention to the newcomer than to us.

If we had food in our hands, we received the attention. Sometimes I put a little grain in my hand when I caught a llama. It was a mixture of corn, barley, and oats, held together with molasses. We called it llama granola, and it was as popular with our llamas as human granola was with us.

One woman who came to visit was captivated. "I had

Combing Posey's wool. The South American cap has a llama design, but the ears are Posey's.

no idea llamas were so approachable," Char said, as Posey blew on her cheek.

"Would you like to help me comb her?" I asked, feeling a little like Tom Sawyer with the bucket of whitewash. I had been meaning to comb her for weeks.

"I'd love to!" said Char, and so we did, using a dog brush to pull out the loose wool, stuffing it into our pockets. We took turns combing, while the other one diverted Posey with nuzzles and kisses. Her wool was long and soft; it was a pleasure to sink a hand down into her thick coat.

In the dusk, we strolled up to the ridge with Posey. The lights of cars on the freeway about a mile away caught her eye, and she stopped. She watched them with great interest. We continued up to the top of the ridge, and she stood erect, silhouetted against the pink sky and distant mountains. Her attention was still on the lights. My attention was on her, my heart full of appreciation for this regal being.

Reward time. Posey goes for the granola.

4

Getting to Know Them

The summer days were long and warm, but winter was already blowing a chill across our minds. Our first winter on the land had been difficult, with the winds battering our trailer as if the thin walls (built in southern California) were gauze curtains. Ice had formed at night on the dogs' water bowl in the kitchen. We had been snowbound a couple of times. For weeks there had been six-foot snowdrifts in Posey's yard. Everyone had said it was the worst winter in years, but we wanted to be well prepared for whatever the coming winter might bring.

We built sheds for the llamas. We moved our trailer to a less exposed spot, and began building a greenhouse attached to the trailer. We worked long hours, enjoying the work and seeing progress.

I was sorry to move the trailer. I had grown accustomed to seeing Levi looking in our bedroom window early in the morning. It was a nice routine, and I would miss it.

But I agreed that the new trailer location was better. Kelly moved the trailer himself, towing it behind our pickup truck. It did seem to fit well into the new spot, still near the llama yards but on the other side of them.

The first morning there, I opened my eyes and looked out the window. Levi and Tumbleweed were sitting in their yard as close to our bedroom window as they could get. Levi was gazing in. I was delighted, even though I recognized that their interest in our movements stemmed, in part at least, from a desire for breakfast.

While I was very fond of Levi, he could exasperate me. Sometimes he was balky on our walks. One evening, we took him out with Posey, leaving Tumbleweed behind. Levi didn't like leaving his buddy, and after a while he just sat down. He wouldn't budge. I tried running at him, which is supposed to get a sitting llama up, but he was imperturbable.

I ran at him again and again, but with no luck. Kelly and I grumbled at him. I started to walk back toward the field where Tumbleweed was watching. Levi immediately stood up and followed me.

We just took him back. All we wanted that evening was a lazy stroll, so we took Posey by herself. "We'd better do more training with Levi," I suggested as we wandered along Llama Lane.

"How do you propose we teach him to do what we want, instead of whatever he pleases?" asked Kelly wryly.

"I don't know. Just practice, I guess."

With every practice session we learned something. Kelly helped me devise a way to hold Posey when I was combing out her wool, one arm around her neck, bracing my body against hers. This steadied both Posey and me. It was a good technique for her, because she liked more body contact than the males did.

My confidence increased as I succeeded in little things. One evening when Kelly led Posey, and I had both males, the tarp covering the tractor flapped in the breeze and startled Posey. She reared up, and the males ran sideways. Levi headed off to the right, while Tumbleweed angled more forward. I held on tight, spinning around with their leads in my hands, ready to let go if I really had to, but delighted and relieved when they stopped and I was still there.

My love for the llamas increased as I became more comfortable around them. Yet at times I felt frustrated: here were these incredibly woolly animals, and I just wanted to cuddle them. Posey liked a cuddle now and then, but you had the challenge of catching her first. The males were not into cuddles.

I had to face it, llamas just weren't teddy bears. They didn't crave the human touch the way many dogs and cats did. Aside from touching noses, llamas touched each other rarely. When they did, it was in fighting or breeding, or it was a mother with a baby. They might crowd each other a bit at the feeding station, but snuggling up was not a joy to a llama.

I was reading, Llama Training: Who's in Charge? at the time, and it called llamas companionable rather than affectionate. That struck me as an apt description. Our three enjoyed being around us. They watched whatever we were doing. Their curiosity seemed endless. They liked walking with us, we knew, as their entire bodies would express interest: ears forward, heads turning from side to side, tails perhaps lifted a little.

I wanted to learn more about relating to them as companions. We did a lot of communicating by looks. I had wondered if looking a llama in the eye would have the aggressive overtones it can with a dog. It seemed that it could at times, but there was a lot of eye contact going on between the llamas and us, and none of our three seemed to take offense. The times of eye

Levi and Tumbleweed.

contact seemed to me times of communion, but I didn't know if the llamas interpreted them in the same way. In exasperation, I wrote:

LEVI AND I

We see
eye to eye.
I cry
oh Levi
why
can't we talk?
We can only walk,
walk and look,
and
see eye to eye.

I recited it to him, in the new barn. He listened. At least he didn't tell me I should have tried iambic pentameter.

Some of my most peaceful moments were the ones I spent alone with the animals. Long afternoons passed dreamily, while I worked in the garden or cleared brush, looking up now and then to watch a llama or look at subtle changes in the mountain view.

On a sunny afternoon, I pulled nails out of old barn wood, working right next to Posey's yard. The old wood was from an early settler's shanty, now collapsed in the valley below us, too fragile to use for anything but decoration. We were going to cover Posey's shed with it. Kelly and Ajila were in town. The sun was warm, but the wind had a bite to it. Distant Mount Shasta was showing white further down her flanks than she had before the recent rains.

My mind gradually loosened up, and in the late afternoon there came over me a delicious sensation of being totally in the present, feeling in harmony with the llamas and the mountains, in harmony even with the stubborn nails. It was a familiar experience, though rare. I usually felt it when I was home alone and outside, frequently in the late afternoon. It may be what makes people into devoted gardeners.

Cider was running around, Martha lying up against

Posey's fence. Posey was sitting near me, watching me carry boards. The cat walked by. In my serene state, I wondered about telepathic communication with animals. I believed that it existed. My experiences of it were limited to a few times when one of our dogs responded to my thoughts. Even then I was reluctant to say that it was telepathy, for possibly I had given clues without realizing it.

Occasionally I experienced telepathic connections with other people. I hadn't tried to develop any skill at doing so, largely because of a reluctance to invade others' privacy. I felt no such reluctance toward the llamas. But if I were to try tuning into them, would there be a way I could know whether I was imagining something, or whether I was really sensing what a llama was experiencing? I didn't know. Llamas were so very different from humans.

In college, I majored in anthropology because of my fascination with the varied ways of life that humans have developed. My interest in llamas stemmed from the same root, a branch further out on the same tree. I didn't want to go way out on a limb, but I kept thinking, what is it like to be a llama?

When I studied anthropology, I saw how easy it was to project the attitudes of one's own culture onto people in other cultures. So too I could see that it would be easy to attribute human characteristics to the llamas.

Yet there was a lot of common ground. Many of their experiences were similar to ours: the pleasure of eating, the importance of companionship, feelings of fear, curiosity, aggression.

Observing llamas, and reading about the observations of other people, was how we had learned most of what we knew about them. I wasn't eliminating the possibility of telepathy, but for now I wanted to focus on what I could observe. We already knew that llamas had a number of ways of communicating. We heard them use a variety of sounds. We saw that head, neck, and tail positions had meanings.

Humming, clicking, snorting and the alarm call were the sounds we had come to recognize. Levi and Tumbleweed had hummed on the ride home. A hum could range from an inquisitive high-pitched squeal to a low grunt. If we separated our two males, Tumbleweed would call to Levi in almost a bleat. "What's going on? Where are you? Huh?" were perfectly contained in the sound.

Posey often hummed when she was sitting in her yard next to a pile of hay, perhaps nosing around in it. She made a soft sound, and seemed contented. Levi sometimes made a sound like that, only greater in volume, if he had been staked out for some time. When he wanted to go back to his yard, he could be very persistent in humming, and you understood that he wanted something.

Clicking and snorting were other llama sounds. So far, only Posey had made them. She did so when she and the males were posturing to each other. When she made these sounds, she stood up very tall, and sometimes put her ears back.

Posey was the most likely to give the alarm call. The first time she did, I was reading in the trailer, Cider on the floor beside me. We both heard a strange sound, a cross between a donkey's bray and a loud hiccup. Cider jumped up, began barking enthusiastically, and running in every direction. I let her out, found some shoes, and followed.

All three of the llamas were looking toward the paved road. Just as I came out, the sound happened again. Cider ran in circles, excited by it. I discovered it came from Posey, who was moving around in prancing steps. An unfamiliar dog was standing on the road, where the llamas were looking. I assumed the intruder was the cause of the alarm, given Posey's history with dogs.

Whenever I heard an alarm call, I went out to investigate. But often I couldn't tell what Posey had seen. Was her vision better than mine, or were we just interpreting things differently? Once it appeared that a large crow had set her off.

On a warm, moonlit night around two in the morning, Posey gave an alarm call. Cider yapped. Posey called again, and Cider echoed it. I looked out and saw Posey's white neck as she moved about. I curled back up next to Kelly, who had barely moved.

Posey gave another alarm call, louder and longer. That did it; I put on a robe and went out. I could see nothing but three llamas and many mountains in the moonlight, but it was pleasant to be out in the quiet night. I was glad for my tomato plants that it was so warm. "Posey, I don't know what you saw," I told her, and went back in. I curled my nicely cooled body around Kelly, and slept till morning.

Another time the call interrupted my writing. "Posey, I'd better tell you the old folk tale about the boy who cried wolf," I grumbled as I went outside. But this time it wasn't Posey.

Tumbleweed was giving the alarm call, and several large cows were walking up our driveway. It was open range in the area, and the cattle were moving up into the cooler elevations. We really didn't want cattle on our land, as they could damage the several hundred small trees Kelly had planted in the spring. We ran down to chase them off, and applauded Tumbleweed for being a good watch-llama.

Of all the posturing, I found ears the most expressive. When our llamas were looking at something in the distance, they moved their ears forward. When we brought them some grain, the forward ears showed interest. When they were listening to something, sometimes one ear was forward and another one back.

Like horses and perhaps other animals, llamas put their ears back as a sign of displeasure or aggressive intent. The two males communicated through slight changes in ear position. In one exchange, Levi's ears were back a little as Tumbleweed approached where Levi was eating. Levi's ears lowered an inch. Tumbleweed didn't leave. Levi lowered his ears further and raised his neck. Tumbleweed left.

Through signals such as these, the two of them worked out their living arrangements. Their system seemed to have some advantage over human ways of handling the same issues. I began indicating my mood by placing my hands at the side of my head in the appropriate position.

There were tail movements which accompanied the ear activities. A tail just hanging down was normal. If a llama felt the need for self-assertion, the tail would go up. The further up, the more aggressive the stance was becoming--until a curious reversal occurred. If the llama flipped his tail all the way over, so that it was resting on his back, that indicated submission.

Levi and Tumbleweed bad mouthing after a spitting match.

Sometimes the llamas didn't come to a peaceful arrangement, and the next escalation could be spitting. The contents of the mouth might be tossed out, or it might be a spray of saliva. Most of the spitting we saw between Lee and Tee--and there wasn't much of it--occurred over food. In the most drastic form of spitting, a llama spat the cud, which was quite smelly, rather like rotten compost. If things became that serious, the llamas would stand around afterwards with their mouths hanging open, airing them out. We called this bad mouthing.

We had seen enough other llamas to know that ours were typical in being moderate about spitting. People who hadn't been around llamas seemed to expect more spitting. It seemed that llamas had been given some undeserved bad press.

Sometimes the two males would chase each other around for a while, nipping at each other. We heard a new sound: Tumbleweed would sometimes screech. It was almost a whinny. They would fight for a while, and then, with no obvious conclusion, the fight would be over and they were buddies again. They fought almost every day for fifteen or twenty minutes.

How much of their behavior was learned, and how much was innate? We had seen a three-hour-old baby at the Patterson's ranch, and he was using the ear movements in exactly the same way adults did. That suggested that much of the behavior was inborn.

We loved watching the llamas and trying to make sense of their actions. Bill Franklin, a wildlife ecologist and owner of llamas and guanacos, had just contributed an article called "Lama Language" to Llama World. He gave names to a variety of body positions and sounds. "Aha, I just saw a HET!" I would exclaim. HET was short for horizontal ear threat, and we noticed it often. The more sensitive we became, the more subtleties we saw. The Aymaran Indians of Lake Titicaca called llamas 'speechless brothers.' We were realizing how very talkative they were.

Levi demonstrates a HET, or horizontal ear threat.

5

Shopping Trip

"WANTED: Distinctly small female(s), long wool, good disposition," ran the ad we placed in Llama World. We were looking for another female or two. It would take a number of years to develop a line of small llamas, if we could do it at all; we were eager to try. Much as we loved Posey, she wasn't really tiny. Her lovely looks and long wool would be assets in our herd, though.

After many years when our savings account rarely exceeded $100, we were slightly astonished to find ourselves able to afford female llamas. Real estate was the reason. We had sold our place in California for far more than it had cost us seven years earlier, and my family home in Washington, D.C., had been sold, with part of the proceeds coming to me. We felt a responsibility to use this money wisely. Late-night talks about it all had ultimately boiled down to developing our land and llamas.

So we were in the right mood when we heard of two small llamas for sale, one a female and one a male. We didn't think we needed another small male yet, but we had heard about this llama. He was at Dan Schoenthal's. All black with a white nose, Whiskers was several inches shorter than Posey, very intelligent, and already trained. The female might be interesting, but I had to have a look at Whiskers.

Our most urgent autumn chores were done: the llama sheds were built, water lines buried, firewood collected, driveway graveled. It was late October, and still Indian Summer, a lovely time for a trip. We cleaned up our old van, found a llama-sitter, and headed north.

We took Cider along. She perched happily between us

on the engine cover, looking out the window at everything. She was a year old now, and beginning to grow out of her puppy excesses.

Indian Summer gave way to Oregon drizzle as we entered the green Willamette Valley. Our first stop was at Safley's, a llama ranch we hadn't seen before. They had the small female. Sally had told us that we would like their place, but she hadn't described it.

It was an enchanted forest. "You'll recognize the place by a llama statue out front," Ken Safley had told me on the phone. The large statue was set in an open field, and suggested that this was no ordinary ranch. Behind the field was woodland, and flitting about among the trees we could see the delicate shapes of dozens of llamas. The continuing rain made the place seem all the more magical: with no clues from the sun, we were suspended outside of time.

Ken gave us a tour, beginning with the forest. Surrounded by beautiful female llamas was the bushy-eyebrowed stud, John L. Lewis. The herd was graceful, mostly medium-sized, with long wool. They were friendly, but stand-offish enough that you could walk easily among them. "I don't like a herd that crowds you," Ken said.

It was fairyland with practical touches. The trees were wrapped with wire, to keep the llamas from eating the bark and killing the trees. There were two latches on the gate between pastures. "That way, if I should ever miss one, the other will hold," Ken pointed out, as we moved into the next field.

Here were the little ones, six months and younger, with their mothers. The woods sloped down to a creek, very full this rainy day. A rounded footbridge led to more pasture. Ken showed us the mother and the grandmother of the little female he had for sale.

Finally we came to her. She was in a large, open barn, with a group of newly-weaned six-month-old babies. She was eleven months old, and shorter than any of them, though more filled out. We walked among the babies. They ran this way and that, continuous movement swirling around us. The one we came to see was standing still, watching us.

She had inherited her father's bushy eyebrows, I was

pleased to see. I liked her looks: a nice straight back and thick, wavy wool. And she was so very small. "She'll grow more," said Ken, "but both of her parents are on the small side. She's not going to be a big llama."

We continued through the grounds, passing a gazebo and going through a gate that brought us out to the back lawn. There was our van, with Cider looking out the window. In the door stood a chow, its blue tongue showing as it barked at Cider. Ken quieted the dog, and invited us in for tea.

We sat by the fire with Ken and his wife Marge, and talked of llamas. They had owned llamas for nine years, and it all started by chance. They stopped for breakfast in the town of Sisters, in eastern Oregon, and drove past the Patterson ranch, which even then had a large llama herd. One thing led to another, and they soon found themselves the owners of Bonnie and Clyde. "They're grandparents to that small one you looked at," Marge said.

Ken liked our idea of breeding small llamas. "Llamas are a great project for kids," he said. "Last year I judged some 4H kids who had trained llamas. Small ones would be good for pets."

I was in the habit of asking llama breeders for their opinions about llamas as an investment. Where most cattle or sheep ranchers I've met would sigh or swear about their financial prospects, llama breeders tended to smile.

Ken smiled. "Oh, I think they'll continue to be an excellent investment," he said. "Suppose you kids got to the point where you could sell a pair of babies a month. Build up your herd a while, and look where you can be in ten years' time." His words cheered me.

The Safleys were so hospitable that we stayed for hours, absorbing information, swapping tales. We were to give them a call the next day, or come by, if we wanted to buy the little female. As soon as we started driving, Kelly said, "We'd be crazy not to buy her."

"I wish I liked her face better," I said.

"I liked it," Kelly said. "She's got character. Did you notice how still she was once we caught her? She's a pretty calm cookie."

"I'm glad I don't have to decide this very minute," I

said.   "I'll probably be clearer in the morning."   The
Safley's place would be right on our way home the next
day.

By the time we arrived at Dan's place, it was well
after dark and raining hard.   He was willing to go out
with a flashlight and find Whiskers, so the three of us
ran through the fields to the barn.   It was very dark.
The rain was finding its way down my neck, my feet
finding their way from one puddle to the next.   The
outside light shone dimly on huddled llama shapes.

Dan brought us into his barn, an old two-storied one,
with a trap door to nether regions.   He left us there
while he went to find Whiskers.

It was almost Halloween. "What a great place for a
spooky party," I said, peering down through the trap
door.   "I wonder what's down there."   The rain on the tin
roof was suddenly softer, and we could speak in normal
tones.

"I'm really curious about this llama," I said to Kelly,
who already knew it.   "I hope his wool is long enough.
Everything else I've heard about him sounds wonderful."

"I love the look of black llamas," said Kelly. "Maybe I
should go out and help Dan."   The rain began coming down
harder, louder on the roof again, and we saw an
approaching flashlight.

The Halloween mood continued as a door banged open,
and a shape entered, all black except for a bit of white
in front.   It shook, and revealed itself as a wet llama.
"Whiskers, I presume," said Kelly.

Whiskers roamed around the barn.   Another llama
wandered in, this one much larger.   Dan came last.   "It
took me a while to lure them in," he said.   "That's
Whiskers, of course,"

"He already introduced himself," I said.

"This one is Kemo," Dan continued.   Kemo was a giant
next to Whiskers.   "I brought him in for contrast."

Whiskers was about Tumbleweed's height, but more
delicately boned.   The tip of his nose and mouth was
white; everything else black.   In the dim light of the
barn, he looked very black.

"You say he's trained?" Kelly asked.

"Yes, he leads very well.   I took him to the state fair,
and he was very good there among all the crowds.   Here,

I'll show you." Dan put a rope on Whiskers, and led him around the barn. "Whiskers, sit down," he said, with a slight tug downward on the lead rope.

Whiskers sat down on the board floor. "I wish now that I hadn't, but I gelded Whiskers' father. His mother died last year. So one good thing about Whiskers as a breeder is that he won't have a bunch of close relatives running around."

Dan handed me the rope. "Tell him 'up,' and pull a little upward," he instructed. I did, and found myself face to face with one alert llama. I led Whiskers around the barn, carefully skirting the open trap door. Dan and Kelly were discussing barn construction.

I liked Whiskers. "You're a real charmer," I said to him. "Do you think you'd like to come live with us?" Whiskers was listening to me. I felt more like the job applicant than like the employer. "Yes, Whiskers, if you come live with us we'll take you hiking. You'll live with a couple of other males, and next year you can breed Posey. Did you ever meet her? She used to live here."

I couldn't tell what he thought of my offer. Kelly walked him around a bit, and we all prepared to leave, the humans to talk in Dan's kitchen, the llamas to go out into the dark night again. I knew they had shelter out there; Dan had explained that they didn't always choose to use it. We had already noticed that with our three at home.

Dan invited us to bring Cider into his house, but her interest in his cats made for too much activity. We put her on the covered porch, and settled down to talk.

I was trying to articulate a recurring question. "I keep wondering what I'm doing with llamas. It's exciting and all that to go around looking at them, and they're fun to have at home, but I wonder if it isn't going to turn out to be just another passing fancy."

"Being around llamas tends to be addicting," Dan said with a grin.

"Yes, I can feel that, but I'm vaguely uncomfortable with my 'back-to-the-land' impulses. Oh, it's wonderful to have a garden, and I do love our land and the llamas, but sometimes I'm afraid of missing out on the really important things, of not making any significant contribution with my life.

"I'm not sure I'm saying what I mean," I continued. "My classmates from Stanford are distinguished professors by now, doing research. Or they're fairly high up in the government. Or combining motherhood with a full-time pediatric practice. And what am I doing? Breeding llamas. This is the twentieth century, this is the nuclear age, this is a time of incredible challenges, and I just wonder if I'm retreating from the real issues by taking on llamas."

Kelly was watching me thoughtfully. We had talked about this before.

Dan told us why he was involved with llamas, breeding them, training them, studying them, brokering them, even planning a trip to South America. "I think there's a lot of significant work that can be done with llamas. They have an important place in healing the breach between man and nature.

"I see what happens on every pack trip we take. Everybody relaxes during the trip. You might expect that just from being out in nature. But it's more than that: people notice the sensitivity and intelligence of the llamas, and it blows their minds. They start thinking about all kinds of things. You wouldn't believe some of the conversations we have, on those llama trips. I've been told many times that they have had a profound impact.

"Humanity must come to a greater appreciation of nature, and it must happen pretty fast," he went on. "If not, well, there's a point of no return out there someplace. If we blow it, it won't be just for ourselves. I'm not doing all this for people. I'm doing it for the llamas."

"Dan, thank you," I said. "You've just handed me a missing piece of my own personal jigsaw puzzle. Not that I'm going to start doing all the things you're doing. For some reason I'm pretty optimistic about the future of our planet. But what you've said gives me more of a feeling for how my enjoyment of llamas could be the basis for something. If this sounds vague, it is. But food for thought."

It was late, and we went out to sleep in our van. As we lay there listening to the rain, I thought of times I had heard the rain on the van in Guatemala. I thought of the harmony with nature of the Indians there, and I thought of the large amounts of pesticide they breathed in the coffee plantations. Nothing was simple. But I had a new piece of the puzzle. Thoughts of llamas turned into dreams of llamas. Whiskers was telling me things.

When we woke, it was still overcast but not actually raining. We took our tea out to the pasture to watch Whiskers. We thoughtlessly brought along the bran muffins we were having for breakfast, and a dozen curious llamas would gladly have relieved us of them. It seemed somehow rude to eat in front of them, so we retreated to the van to finish breakfast.

Whiskers was small, dark, and handsome among Dan's males.

We scarcely had to discuss it; both of us felt Whiskers would be a fine addition to our little herd. Kelly rearranged the van, tying the table top so that Cider could be kept up front with us, and Whiskers could ride with more space in back. Kelly needed to putter with the engine too.

I went back to the llama pasture, taking Cider with me on lead. I wanted to watch Whisker's interactions with the larger males. Dan had said Whiskers could be quite a fighter, one who wouldn't hesitate to take on llamas much larger than himself.

Nobody was fighting this morning. Cider wanted to play with the llamas. To distract her, I walked her around the large pasture, letting her sniff this and that, a bush here, a dung pile there.

At first the llamas watched us from afar. Then they all came running across the meadow, Whiskers in the lead, Kemo a close second. We made quite a procession, meandering around the yard at a dog's pace. Whenever Cider would turn toward the llamas, they stepped back a little. When she turned away, they came up closer.

Dan joined me there. "Kelly said you've decided to take Whiskers," he said, and I felt that he was glad. "Be sure and take him places, do things with him, or he'll be bored. He loves to have a good time."

Whiskers went willingly into our van, and we drove back to Safley's. Ken was out, and Marge let us take our time. We looked at the small female's parents and the two grandparents that were there. Kelly was ready to buy her, but I still needed to think more.

I sat for a while by myself in the pen with the little one and the young weanlings. They were restless and humming, perhaps because they had recently been removed from their mothers. She was quiet, watching me in a relaxed way. We made eye contact for several long, hypnotic seconds, and I felt that I was seeing her soul in her dark eyes. I liked her.

I roamed around, trying to find what my reluctance was. Was my intuition trying to tell me something? The footbridge across the creek beckoned, and I sat there, dangling my legs over the side. Aha! Spending that much money was bothering me: even though we had planned to do it, parting with thousands of dollars was not easy.

Once I realized it, I laughed. A little anxiety wasn't going to stop me from buying this llama. I imagined how it would be to have her in our herd, and it felt lovely. As I stretched and looked up, a young llama was romping across the meadow, nice symbol of fecundity and increase.

"Well, I'm finally ready," I murmured to myself, and went to find Kelly.

Loading the struggling young one in the van was a job, but soon we had both llamas settled. We tied Whiskers up, just in case he decided to try breeding the new one.

Whiskers had been humming interrogatively, but once we loaded the female, he was quiet. On the front seat, Cider was shaking with curiosity.

The new female stood up for more of the trip than Whiskers did. The only rough part of the drive was going through Eugene during rush hour, having to zig and zag through unfamiliar streets on our way to the freeway. The llamas tended to bump as we turned right or left.

We stopped for a quick dinner after dark. As we sat eating hamburgers in a busy fast food place, I watched the outlines of the llamas as they moved around in the van. Whiskers bumped the back light switch on, so it was easy to see the two new members of our family.

We arrived home late at night, in a drizzle. By flashlight we unloaded the little one into Posey's yard. Posey came racing over making loud clicking and snorting noises. Levi and Tumbleweed always responded to Posey's clicking with their low-rider posture, but this young female lifted her tail and stood up straight. She and Posey sniffed each other. "Posey, meet Lil Bit," I said.

Whiskers greets Lil Bit and Posey on his first morning at Juniper Ridge Ranch.

I led the new one into the shed, and took her lead off. She noticed the hay. Then I leaned against the juniper tree and watched while the two females got acquainted. Posey followed the newcomer around, sometimes clicking. Lil Bit didn't make any sounds.

Kelly led Whiskers into the males' yard. Smelling noses and rears was the main activity over there too. It was all very amicable. We hadn't really known what to expect.

The rain increased, and we went inside. The first llama I saw in the morning was Whiskers, looking in our bedroom window. Tumbleweed and Levi soon wandered out from the barn, large Levi lurking in a submissive pose behind Tumbleweed. Whiskers strolled the perimeter of the yard, gazing out in every direction, but specially at the females. He looked right at home.

6

Winter Tales

On a chilly afternoon late in the fall, we staked out
the three males on the slope below the females' yard.
There was much clucking and tail movement as we tied
them up, but soon the males ignored Posey and Lil Bit.
They settled down to the serious business of eating.

Kelly went off to town, and I did outdoor chores,
twice untangling Whiskers when he wrapped his lead rope
around a small tree. I harvested the last of the
Jerusalem artichokes, and put the garden to bed for the
winter. I took manure from the females' yard, and
spread it on the beds. The gate latch was a little
awkward, and I was careful to make sure it caught.

I went back for more manure. After latching the gate
I rubbed Lil Bit's neck. "You're so approachable," I told
her, "so easy to catch. Don't you like it when I scratch
your neck hard?" She liked it, and stretched her neck
out luxuriously.

I looked up and saw that Posey was browsing just
outside the gate. Somehow it had swung open. I heard
myself say, "Oh no."

I tied Lil Bit up, and sat down, hoping--but not really
expecting--that Posey might just wander back in. My
heart was pounding. I was mad at myself for not being
more careful. I took several deep breaths and thought
about what I could do. I tried not to think about the
story I had read in the 3L Llama about two llamas that
were lost for a couple of weeks. That was from a pack
trip, not their own yard--and they had eventually turned
up.

Soon Posey wandered away from the gate. I could
imagine her walking back into the yard after exploring

the big world for a while, so I put a bucket with some grain just inside the gate, where it might arouse her curiosity.

Posey was having a good time browsing and wandering among the three tied-up males. I decided I would break it up if they tried to breed, but it didn't advance beyond flirtation. After the first couple of minutes, I decided that Posey wasn't about to take off into the rapidly approaching sunset.

After following her around for half an hour, never getting close, I had to admit that I had no idea how to catch her. My pockets were stuffed with grain, and I had a lead rope around my waist, but Posey wasn't letting me anywhere near her. I had never lassoed anything in my life.

I wanted help. Maybe I could find a neighbor at home, but I preferred Kelly. Darkness was only a couple of hours away, and I didn't like the idea of Posey loose in the dark. I ran into the trailer, and phoned the place where Kelly was planning to jam with the High Street Boogie Band. He wasn't expected there for a while yet, but the guitarist promised to send him home if I hadn't called back.

I grabbed a camera and a roll of film before going back out. Posey was grazing midway between the trailer and the other llamas, and she watched me while I sat on the ground and loaded the camera.

We were each keeping an eye on the other. "Hey Posey, am I part of your herd?" I asked.

She began roaming further afield, gradually making her way up toward the ridge, occasionally checking to make sure I was nearby. I stayed back; I didn't want my presence encouraging her to go farther.

For the first time she moved out of sight of the other llamas, following a deer trail that led out to a rocky point. She certainly was having an adventure, and she seemed to be enjoying it thoroughly. Now that I had the camera in my hand, I was enjoying myself a little more too. I photographed her just as she was silhouetted against a bend in the path. She disappeared from my sight, and I felt nervous again.

Then she was above me, at the top of the ridge. Suddenly she took off and ran, a beautiful frisky run, all

About to disappear from view, Posey explores the ridge.

the way down the slope to the other llamas. I galloped after her, with perhaps a little less grace. She sniffed noses with Lil Bit, and browsed near the males. I strolled around, noticing my cold toes and nose. The sun was down.

It was a relief to hear the sound of our truck. I filled Kelly in on Posey's activities, and filled his pockets up with grain. Posey was flirting with the males again. "She even sat down for Levi a while ago," I told Kelly, "but he didn't take advantage of it."

"She's sure ready to breed. We won't have any trouble when the time comes," he said.

Posey had noticed Kelly. He offered her a handful of grain but while she was thinking about it, Levi ate it. She came closer, and Kelly gave her several handfuls. He tried to grab her. She stepped back.

Then she was between her gate and a woodpile. Kelly came toward her, so that she either had to go into her yard or go right past him. I was behind him. She glanced at us and walked into her yard.

We later thought of a way I could have caught her by myself. "If you had taken one of the males into her yard and tied him up, he might have acted as a lure," Kelly said. "Or all three," I added. We agreed that all three males tied up in her yard would have been irresistible.

For weeks afterward, Posey watched the gate closely. She didn't know we had put two latches on it.

"Were you scared?" Kelly asked me when we talked it over.

"Well, a little. But after the first few minutes, I realized she would stay close. Remember when we talked about raising llamas, this is the kind of thing I thought I couldn't handle. And I'm sure glad you did come home. But it probably would have been okay anyway."

Winter came early. It began snowing in November, and it didn't stop. The snow piled up higher and higher, until only the top two feet of the six-foot llama fences were visible. Kelly spent hours on the tractor, clearing our long driveway. After a while, he just gave up. We parked our car, our truck, and the tractor down by the paved road, about a quarter of a mile away. We got a lot of exercise bringing groceries in.

I worried about the llamas at first. They had no polypropylene underwear, no down comforters. But when I put my hand deep into Tumbleweed's wool, I was comforted. It might not be down, but that wool was covering a warm body. Did the llamas get cold feet and noses? They tucked their feet under their bodies when they sat, and they didn't really seem to mind the cold. I knew of other llama breeders who kept llamas in colder conditions than ours. Since llamas were native to the Andes up to 14,000 feet, they must be well adapted to cold. They were quite a contrast to Cider. Our dog of African heritage growled when forced away from the wood stove.

When the snow finally let up, I dug a path in the males' yard. There was about three feet of snow, but the wind had blown it into high and low spots. The snow came up to my shoulder where I began digging the path. It was light enough that the digging was easy, and with a big snow shovel it went quickly. I dug a winding path out to a loop, so they could chase each other without having to back out. Levi, then Tumbleweed, came out to watch me. Levi went back into the barn, but Tumble stayed out with me. I talked to him when I had the breath.

Tumbleweed on a path in the snow.

We dubbed the path Llama Loop, and Kelly began putting some hay out there. We had cold but clear weather for weeks, and the llamas went out there much of every day. On a windy morning, with the temperature at nine degrees Fahrenheit, Whiskers sat out there for hours, eating hay, looking as comfortable as if it were spring.

We had built llama sheds with open doorways. Because we had heard that llamas didn't like dark buildings, on the roofs we installed corrugated fiberglass roofing, alternating in strips with the metal, to let more light in the sheds during the day.

Our llamas seemed to like their sheds. From our bedroom window we could see the door to the females' little shed. Posey would often sit in the doorway, looking out, and Lil Bit would be further in. The large juniper near their door combined with the wind patterns to provide Posey and Lil Bit with a patch of bare ground. Often they would walk around or sit out there.

The close quarters tried their patience at times. "The walls of the girls' shed are covered with green globs," Kelly reported one day after feeding. "Looks like they had a long spitting match."

At other times, non-violent methods worked. We watched Lil Bit approach the shed when Posey was blocking the doorway. Posey stood with her ears back. It was clear she didn't want to let Lil Bit into the shed, where the fresh hay had just been piled. Lil Bit stood by the door, her back to Posey, and inched her way in. She slowly crowded against Posey until both llamas were in the shed. Then she turned around for breakfast.

Whiskers, Tumbleweed, and Levi on Llama Loop.

I saw less of the llamas, and I missed them. Most of my attention was on work in town. One evening, I was teaching a class in self-hypnosis for writing. The students were sitting with eyes shut, absorbed in the task I had given them, of allowing a symbol to arise from the inner mind. It could be anything, and it was to help them with writing. I sat quietly.

Suddenly I felt a symbol inside me too, so I closed my eyes and relaxed. There was Tumbleweed, close up, looking at me with his clear gaze, so very dignified even with the perpetual wisp of hay dangling from his mouth. "Write for us!" his gaze said to me. "Tell people who we are."

My heart seemed to expand beyond my body, so much love did I feel for him. In that moment he wasn't so much an animal who lived in a fenced yard on my land as he was a wise benefactor, serene yet needing what I could give. I felt respect for him and for his wisdom. When it came to writing a book, he was truly a speechless brother. For that he needed me.

Our Christmas card, a sketch Kelly did, with the five llamas playing reindeer.

Our Christmas card was a sketch that Kelly did, with five llamas, the two of us, both dogs and the cat. We received mostly amused comments from friends and relatives, but one uncle of Kelly's wrote, "I envy you the mountains but you can keep the llamas."

"He must not know how delightful they are," I said when Kelly read the card aloud. "Probably thinks they spit a lot or something."

Kelly had never been spat upon. "Do they spit at you?" asked a reporter who was doing a llama story for a Portland paper.

"Oh no," Kelly said cheerfully. "They do spit at each other now and then, but not at us."

"How long is their wool?" asked the photographer. Kelly was holding Lil Bit, and he parted the strands of her wool. Lil Bit turned her head around and spat. First she hit the photographer; next, the writer; then Kelly felt a little pop-pop-pop as the grain he had just given her landed on his forehead. Luckily the visitors believed Kelly's protestations that this was rare, and didn't feature spitting in the article.

When the llamas spat whatever was in their mouths at the time, it had little smell. At other times, when they were more riled, they brought up their cud. That could smell rancid. Lil Bit once bestowed a smelly spit on me. I had just washed my hair, but I headed for the shower again.

Kelly and I celebrated New Year's Eve with a bottle of champagne by the fire. Just before midnight we went down to the barn for a party. Our footsteps and flashlights woke the llamas up. Tumbleweed had the cute sleepy look of a small child in the middle of the night. He and the others woke up enough for some grain.

It was a beautiful night, cold and clear, stars filling the sky from one mountain horizon to another. Although there was no moon, the mountains were bright with snow. I thought of the parties in town we had been invited to, and was glad to be home instead. What better way to end the year than with the animal friends who had made it so special? I felt a thrill inside me as I thought of living with llamas in the coming year. I felt a chill inside me as a gust of wind whipped through my down jacket. When we went back inside, it was past midnight. We hadn't heard any horns or firecrackers. We hadn't even kissed, but--better late than never--we took care of that.

We worked outside on New Year's Day. Kelly added beams to the sheds to strengthen them against the snow load, and I dug manure from the females' shed. The heavy work made us warm, and we had a quart jar of orange juice with us. Lil Bit sniffed it over thoroughly.

She sat down by her front door, and watched our activities. I hunkered down next to her and rubbed her neck. "Lil Bit, I bet it would be easy to make you into a pet. You're a bit much for a trailer, but when the greenhouse is built, I'll try bringing you in," I promised. Just before winter set in, we had purchased another trailer of 1950s vintage. Our two trailers were parked in an open-ended V shape. Between them we were building a large greenhouse and living room.

We finished the afternoon's work with a little llama training. We put cinches around Levi and Whiskers, as a step toward packing with them. They moved away from us and threatened with their necks as we put the cinches on, but once they were on, the llamas seemed oblivious to them.

"Sweetie, are you afraid?" Kelly asked, as I passed the cinch under Whiskers' belly.

"Afraid? No, I'm not," I snapped.

"You underrate your strength and skill," Kelly said.

"I'm not underrating it," I replied. "I just don't want to get kicked. But if I can learn to handle llamas probably just about anybody could."

One wintry day, our veterinarian came out on a farm call. The llamas were due for worming and inoculating. We had meant to do it in the fall, but kept putting it off until we decided whether to geld Levi.

Gelding was said to make a male llama more tractable, and since we didn't plan to breed Levi, we thought about it. But he was such a fine fellow that we decided we might change our minds about breeding. He was to remain intact.

Howdy Miller was our vet. He had been recommended to us because he had experience with llamas. I was delighted to find that he also had a natural warmth toward both humans and animals. I wanted a vet who

Lil Bit in the greenhouse living room, as promised.

was comfortable with emotion--if he was there when our old dog Martha died, I wanted to be able to cry without embarrassment. With Howdy, I knew I could.

Kelly held Levi while Howdy put the worming medicine, a paste, in Levi's mouth. I kept the other llamas from crowding around. Levi struggled, and as I watched, I felt my physical uncertainty. What good was Phi Beta Kappa now? If Levi were really carrying on, I'd be scared of being hurt. Kelly had been right that day when we talked. I realized now that I was afraid, and I was embarrassed at being afraid.

Tumbleweed's curiosity brought him closer. Since they were almost finished with Levi, I nabbed Tumble. Usually I could hold on, but this time he really didn't want to be caught. He bolted. I kept my arms around his neck until he darted out the door, but I wasn't dedicated enough to let myself be scraped against the side of the doorway.

So once again my physical strength had been inadequate to hold a llama. But, paradoxically, I felt better. I knew that I could think of other ways to do things. We could build or buy a restraining chute. Sure, there might be an emergency sometime where I would be less skilled than I would want to be, but the number of times that would happen would probably be small. And I would learn from each one. I didn't have to be a 5'3" Superwoman. I'd just be myself, and that would be good enough.

Whiskers came up near me, and I caught him. He didn't resist. When Howdy called for Whiskers, I had him ready.

Howdy demonstrated giving shots, but I didn't absorb much. Many llama breeders did their own worming and inoculating. Later for all that. I was learning step by step, and if the steps were small, so be it. They were steps.

7

The Birds, the Bees, and the Llamas

We had started saying, "We're llama breeders," when we acquired our first female. Now it was time to actually do some breeding. We had waited until early May to breed so the baby would be born in warm weather the following year. We hadn't seen any breeding or any births, so it was all rather abstract.

Our interest in breeding small llamas continued. A geneticist told me that we had chosen a relatively easy thing to breed for. Height was controlled by several genes; the exact number wasn't known. Chances were good that small llamas would reproduce small.

Posey wasn't short, but her offspring by small males might be. Lil Bit had grown some since we bought her, but she was still very small. We heard of a small female for sale in the Midwest. We looked at photos of her, but we decided we didn't want to buy a llama sight unseen or make a trip to the Midwest.

The llamas seemed to be thinking about breeding too. Early in the spring, when we resumed regular llama hikes, we took Levi and Tumbleweed out. After a few mouthfuls of fresh green grass, they ran up to the fence around the females' yard. Immediately the familiar "junior high dance" routine began. Posey and Lil Bit stood very straight and tall, clucking, their tails arched high. Lee and Tee were eagerly touching noses through the fence with the girls, heads moving up and down, all the way to the ground and back up again. The males' posture was more upright than it had been in the fall. Junior high dances had given way to high school.

Whiskers was running around in the males' yard, along the fence nearest the females' yard. He was grimacing.

"Whiskers looks mad," Kelly said.   "He didn't get to go to the dance."

We chose Mother's Day for the first breeding.   It was to be Posey and Whiskers.   We had had many discussions about whom to breed to whom.   Posey was ready. Whiskers was three and a half, so he was full grown. The other males, not quite two, might not be able to breed successfully yet.   I was eager to see a Tumbleweed-Posey baby, as Tumbleweed had such good wool and a more placid disposition than Whiskers, but I agreed that a Whiskers-Posey baby could be wonderful too.

We put Posey in a newly-fenced pasture next to her old one.   Then we brought Whiskers to her.   With the fence between them, they both snorted and stood up tall.   Whiskers' tail wagged rapidly; it seemed to be a gesture of assertiveness.   Kelly led him in, and I closed the gate.   Posey came right up, then retreated.

Whiskers went straight to the females' dung pile.   He spent about ten minutes there, sniffing it thoroughly, then

Posey watches Whiskers performing flehmen at the females' dung pile.

angling his neck up into the air. He was very interested in it.

"An experienced stud will go right to work, but sometimes the young ones get hung up performing flehmen at the dung pile," we had been told by another breeder. Whiskers was supposedly learning from the scent of the pile that there was a female open for breeding. When he seemed to be sniffing the air, a gland at the back of his mouth was operating, decoding the message of the dung pile.

Posey watched him, then came over to sniff the movie camera, which she hadn't seen before. The 35mm camera was familiar, and scarcely warranted a sniff.

They approached each other--"finally!" I said--and Whiskers reared up as if fighting another male. Posey ran away from him. He discovered the lush green grass, much nicer than the grass in his yard, and he grazed his way around the pasture.

"It's cold," I said, as the sun disappeared behind a cloud.

"We could go sit in the van. They wouldn't be able to see us, and it would be warmer," suggested Kelly. Whiskers frolicked across the field.

We settled into the warmer environment of the van. "Junior high dances is right," I grumbled. "She's on one side of the field and he's on the other. I thought they'd just do what comes naturally. Are we going to have to teach them what to do?"

"Whiskers is kind of stand-offish with other llamas," Kelly said. "Maybe it'll just take him a while before he pays much attention to her."

"Then I'll go dig in the garden, and watch from there," I said. "This could take all day."

"Okay," Kelly said. "I'll leave you the cameras. Guess I'll go inside. Call me when something happens."

We walked up toward the garden, closer to the other llamas. Lil Bit, Levi, and Tumbleweed were watching Posey and Whiskers.

I worked for an hour or so in the garden. Nothing much happened. Even the other llamas stopped paying attention. Lil Bit chased the peacocks.

That night Posey and Whiskers slept at opposite ends of the pasture. Every time we looked the next day, they

Lil Bit is curious about our young peacock.

were apart. Gradually the distance between them decreased until they were only ten or twenty feet apart.

After a couple of days of nothing happening, we put Whiskers back in his yard. We remembered hearing that you stood a better chance of breeding if you put the female in with the male.

We did just that the next day, after staking Lee and Tee out where they couldn't see the goings-on. We didn't want to make them jealous, and we wanted to minimize any disturbance among the males.

Then we walked Posey over. Whiskers made lovely gurgling noises in his throat. I recognized them as 'orgling'; Andy Tillman had described the sound in his book, Speechless Brothers.

As soon as Posey was in his yard, Whiskers tried to mount her. We cheered. Posey explored the place, sniffing dung piles. She didn't sit down for him. For several minutes, she strolled around the yard, with Whiskers hanging on behind. Lil Bit was most interested in the proceedings, running around by the fence.

"I guess it's progress," Kelly said. "Since we can see this yard better from the house, let's leave Posey in here for several hours and keep checking."

Whiskers is trying to mount Posey, but she isn't sitting down for him.

So we did. Nothing happened. Late in the afternoon, we put Posey back in with Lil Bit, and brought Lee and Tee home. Whiskers chased them around the yard for a while.

The next day it rained off and on. During one of the nice spells, we took the two younger males out to graze and we put Posey in with Whiskers. As before, he orgled and tried to mount her, and as before, she walked around the yard with him hanging on behind.

We decided that our absence might speed the course of true love, so we went inside to watch from the window. By the time we were at the window, Whiskers was browsing. That was it.

We went outside to remove Posey, planning to bring her back later, but after she was on lead, Kelly and I both had the same idea. What would Whiskers do if Posey were sitting down?

We hadn't trained her to sit down. When I touched her legs, she pranced around, then sat to get away from me. Kelly took a firm hold on her lead. Whiskers came over, and began sniffing around Posey's tail. Posey, startled, jumped up.

A successful breeding at last.

We got her back down, and Whiskers came right back. He began orgling and stepped over Posey, rubbing her sides with his front hoofs. He sat down on her. I quietly let myself out of the llama yard, and ran for the camera. Kelly was still holding Posey's lead.

Finally something was happening. We had given Whiskers plenty of bawdy encouragement these past few days, but that was all we could think of to do. They were supposed to know what to do. Well, it was happening now. I sat down by the strawberry bed and took some pictures of the three of them. I hoped Kelly wasn't too uncomfortable, hunched down, holding Posey's lead, and I wondered how long it took llamas to mate. Forty-five minutes came into my mind from somewhere, but I wasn't sure. At least it had stopped drizzling.

Kelly certainly was in the middle of things. "I was fascinated," he told me later. "Whiskers had a glazed look in his eyes. He seemed off in some other world. and he never stopped orgling. Posey was so incredibly calm. I couldn't believe how calm she was. You know she's usually rather nervous, but she was so peaceful. And affectionate--she just kept nuzzling me, sniffing my pockets and my cap, rubbing my cheeks."

"What about that time when she turned her head up to Whiskers?" I asked.

"I couldn't really tell what that was," Kelly replied. "You saw how he kept trying to bite her ears. She didn't seem to mind that at all. Maybe she just wanted to nuzzle him too."

Posey's rear was glistening. "Looks like the deed is done!" said Kelly.

"Now let's hope for a daughter," I suggested, imagining Posey giving birth easily to a beautiful baby, full term, everything perfect. We had wondered if motherhood might settle Posey's youthful skittishness; this calm was a good sign.

We weren't sure if one breeding would have settled Posey. We decided to try again. Posey sat down for Whiskers without our help. But she didn't lift her tail. We tried to lift it. Whiskers seemed frustrated: he kept getting off Posey, then back on. Sometimes he mounted her backwards, and sat down on her shoulders.

"Next time let's tie a string around her tail," Kelly

suggested. "Then we can pull the tail aside just when Whiskers sits down."

I objected. "If llamas have been in existence for all these years, they must manage to perpetuate the species without help from string."

Kelly convinced me that it would be worth trying. "After all, remember the breeder who put her llama's tail into a French braid? And there was that very woolly llama who never got pregnant until she was sheared. We're just helping nature."

We tried the string technique the next day, and it worked fine. Posey and Whiskers had a good breeding session. We did it another day, also with good results. The llamas were getting the hang of it, but when we tried without the string, that long tail of Posey's was in the way again.

We had another problem. Whenever we brought the two younger males back into the yard with Whiskers after he had been breeding, he was one aggressive llama. He chased them around vigorously, evidently claiming the territory as his. The males had always fought, but this was too much.

We put Posey and Lil Bit into their new pasture, separate from their older, smaller yard. We put Whiskers in there by himself for the breeding season.

Whiskers and Tumbleweed are fighting, and Levi is coming over to watch more closely. Tumbleweed brings Whiskers to his knees, a common fighting move.

Tumbleweed and Whiskers fighting, rearing up so that their chests butt together.

So Posey had been bred. Was she pregnant? Pregnancy tests had become available for llamas just the previous year. You had to wait at least three weeks after breeding. Then you nicked the female's ear with a razor blade, and mailed off some of the blood in a little plastic container.

After the requisite three weeks, we caught Posey, tied her up, and put alcohol on her ears. I made several cuts, but all we got was a drop or two. Kelly felt sick at messing up her ears. I was determined, buoyed up by my desire to learn all about llama care.

We obviously didn't have the technique down. I phoned a friend, and she gave me more detailed instructions. We went back out, but by then I couldn't bring myself to slice up Posey. Kelly made the cut. Same thing: not enough blood.

"This is ridiculous," Kelly said. "Let's try check-breeding. At least it won't cause any pain." If a female who had been bred didn't let a male mount her within four minutes, it often meant she was pregnant.

We put Posey in with Whiskers. She was most unwilling to enter his yard, balking at every step. "Oh good," I said, "maybe that means she's pregnant."

Whiskers tried to mount Posey as soon as he could. She stood looking around, as if there weren't the weight of a male llama on her hindquarters. But after a minute, she sat down. Whiskers went to work.

"Darn it!" I exploded. "I thought llama breeding was easy!"

"How reliable is this check-breeding business?" Kelly asked me.

"I think it's pretty accurate. A lot of breeders use it. But here we are well into the summer, and we don't know if this girl is pregnant." I turned to Whiskers. "If you haven't done the job, fellow, we'll try Tumbleweed. How would you like that?" I knew he'd hate it.

We had to wait another three weeks before we could try the blood test. Neither one of us was willing to slice ears again, so our vet, Howdy Miller, came by.

Posey struggled, but Howdy got a sample from her jugular vein, a procedure recommended only for veterinarians. We sent it off in the mail and I began going to the post office with a sense of anticipation. At last it was there--the envelope from Rocky Mountain Laboratories.

I took the mail out to the car. My heart was pounding. I opened the envelope. Posey was pregnant. "Well, hooray!" I said out loud. "Posey, you're pregnant!" Llama breeding was easy.

8
Catalog and Conference

The late afternoon sun flooded the music room of Bobra and Ulo Goldsmith's home in Boulder, Colorado. It illuminated the grand piano, the patterned Persian rug, the ceiling-high bookshelves filled with art books and works of European authors. Heaped on the rug were llama halters in red, blue, green, brown, and black. On a low table next to them was a pile of thermometers, each with a length of string and a clothes pin attached. A black driving harness was stretched over a chair, on top of saddle pads, trail bells, and curry combs.

I sat on the sofa, writing, my feet propped up on the coffee table next to slides of llamas having their fighting teeth removed. The annual International Llama Association conference was to begin in a few days, and Bobra was chairing it. Already the phone was ringing steadily. After the conference, she would be putting on a llama pack trip into the Rockies. I was helping her put out the equipment catalog for her llama business, Rocky Mountain Llamas, and I would be taking part in the packing.

Afternoon turned to evening as I sat writing, enjoying the balmy June air. Bobra came in, back from finding hay for the llamas who would be attending the conference. She and I put together the catalog, rewriting, doing layout, sometimes letting ourselves get distracted into llama chit-chat. A friend of Bobra's did lettering and drawings, and Bobra's niece Margie wrote up the llama first-aid kit. At one in the morning, we ordered a pizza from a take-out place, and I admitted there were advantages to living in a city. The others left; Bobra and I put the last touches on the layout, less tempted now to distract ourselves with idle talk. The sky was showing a streak of light when we finished, but it was worth it. The catalog would be ready in time for the conference.

"This afternoon we'll go out to the llamas," Bobra promised.

"I'm beginning to feel llama deprivation," I said. "The only llama I've seen since I left home was one that had just been shorn within a half-inch of its skin, on a ranch in Idaho. Poor thing, it wasn't very pretty! I did see some antelope by the railroad tracks in Wyoming, and they were lovely. But they weren't llamas. I never thought I could be a guest in your house for over two days before seeing even one llama!"

"If you want, I'll take you over there right now," Bobra kidded. She could barely keep her eyes open.

"That's okay, this afternoon will be fine. I was thinking of a little siesta now."

We did go out to the llamas late that afternoon. Bobra kept them about three miles from her home, at her parents' place. I knew she had over forty of them, but I wasn't prepared for the effect when she stood in a pasture and called, "Ladies! Ladies!"

A flowing wave of brown began moving in the back pasture and separated itself into individual llamas as they came closer. Some were deep brown, some white, some golden brown, some mixtures of colors. They came in all sizes, and they moved with the graceful motion so characteristic of the llama.

All but one. One small llama was bobbing up and down. She came right up to me, and I could see that she only had one rear leg. "That's Ariel," explained Bobra. "She was born with the top of a femur broken off, and the leg had to be amputated. It's extremely rare for something like this to happen. She's very friendly because she had a lot of medical attention when she was young. We won't breed her; we call her our pet-wool llama. Feel her wool."

It was long and silky. Ariel nuzzled my elbow.

Bobra introduced many of her llamas to me. "This one's Regal, she's the dominant one in the female herd. Here's Greyling, she's one of the pregnant ones due soon. The other very pregnant ones are Copper, over there, and

Motley. It would be fun for you to see a birth while you're here."

I was hoping for it. I had never seen a llama birth, though I had seen slides of what looked liked bagpipes emerging from a female llama. Baby llamas have long, long legs.

I met Bobra's males, kept in several pastures. Handsome had to be kept apart from other males, or he would fight too much over his territory. "You have to know your animals," Bobra said. "Some you can keep together, some you can't."

"I used to keep Hidalgo in with Spook," she added, "until one spring, when I was using Spook a lot for breeding. When he and Hidalgo were alone in the pasture together, he would occasionally mount Hidalgo. One day I went to put Hidalgo away after a hike, and he gave me a look that said clearly, 'Don't put me back in with that maniac!' So I didn't."

Bobra pointed out another llama, Streak, who boarded there. "Last winter I saw him watching the snow come down. It was after dark, and the flakes were illuminated by an outside light on the barn. He stood for the longest time, just looking. You know, sometimes you can practically see wheels turning in their heads." We wandered among the animals, putting out hay and filling water buckets as we went. Then it was back to the bustle of conference preparations.

I went out to the llamas with Bobra every day after that. One morning we worked with Squire.

"He's quite a smart llama," Bobra said, "and something of a brat too. He learns very fast, and then figures out how to avoid any work, if possible. He's challenging to work with."

Squire was a tall, rather slim gelding whom Bobra was planning to enter in the llama parade at the conference. She had already worked with him a number of times, teaching him to wear a driving harness, obey voice and rein commands, and pull a lightweight cart called a sulky.

He clucked his displeasure repeatedly as we caught him and harnessed him. We attached the sulky, and walked him up and down the driveway. His clucks grew more frequent; he began spitting. It wasn't aimed at anybody, and the fine spray just went out in front.

"He's got to learn that he must sometimes do what he doesn't wish to," Bobra said. "That's an important lesson for any llama. They enjoy so much of what you ask them to do, that it can come as a shock to a llama when he realizes you're insisting on something he doesn't want."

Bobra was calm, though occasionally she spoke sternly to Squire, telling him what a naughty boy he was being today, or using a single firm "NO" in a tone that would have stopped most children. It stopped Squire too.

"Llamas learn so quickly compared to horses, it's really a joy to work with them. A lot of what I learned in training horses is useful with llamas too, but they don't need the many repetitions horses do. Now I think we're ready to go out," she added.

We left the ranch and began moving along residential streets. Squire walked steadily, his ears forward with interest. "What a difference," I remarked. "He looks like he's having fun."

"Yes, he loves to see new sights." Bobra moved from walking behind Squire to sitting on the seat of the sulky. He scarcely noticed the change.

Bobra drove him, while I jogged along beside. My job was simply to be an additional control, if needed, while he was getting used to pulling the cart. He was aware of me, but attuned chiefly to Bobra's commands. We covered a couple of miles in a quiet neighborhood, Squire noticing people and dogs before I did. People working in their yards or out jogging called out greetings as we went past.

"Squire did well after that first bit of fussing," Bobra commented. "I'll practice with him early each morning until the parade."

That afternoon the International Llama Association conference began, on the University of Colorado campus. I felt much more at home than I had the previous year. As I helped at the registration desk, I observed that all kinds of people were attending. As I talked with them during the conference, I found they had many reasons for owning llamas. Some were ranchers trying another form of livestock. Some, like Bobra and myself, were fascinated by the process of training llamas and by the relationships we developed with the animals. Others held llamas primarily as an investment. Still others were spinners or weavers, with a central interest in wool. Some were packers. Underlying all these reasons, throughout the conference, I sensed love and respect for the llamas.

That llama breeding is a new field was evident. Someone who had been in it five years was an old-timer already. The International Llama Association itself wasn't that old, nor was the other llama association, LANA (Llama Association of North America). People were passing on training tips, information on feed, news of all sorts. Talks were given on a wide variety of topics, and it was clear that knowledge about llamas was expanding rapidly.

You could hear conversations about llamas and money. There was a consistent attitude expressed at the conference that llamas were good investments. Not surprising, considering the group, but there were differences between this conference and the last one.

At the last conference we had heard of several females for sale. This time, I stopped by a buyers' and sellers' get-together one evening in the lounge. While a few males were for sale, nobody was offering females; they seemed available primarily through waiting lists. Several breeders had already raised their prices substantially, and others were debating whether to follow suit.

The numbers of people wanting llamas were increasing, and rising prices weren't slowing the demand. I heard some figures at a program on marketing: there were approximately 235 million people in the United States, about 130 million cattle, 43 million dogs, 39 million cats, and 11 million horses. So with a llama population of around seven thousand, Dick Patterson said, it seems unlikely that the market will become saturated any time soon. From this and other talks, it was easy to draw the conclusion that llamas were good business as well as good fun.

A day at the county fairgrounds offered both. We spent the morning watching training and veterinary techniques demonstrated on llamas that had been brought to the conference. After lunch, the general public was invited to come see llamas.

A llama parade began. A four year old girl rode a llama. Bobra was in the sulky behind Squire. Another llama carried two large bales of hay, one on either side. There were llamas carrying packs. It was not a long parade, so the llamas and people went around again.

A woman in the crowd behind me said, "I had no idea llamas were so smart. Let's go visit some llama owners some weekend."

Her husband said, "Did you hear how much they cost?"

"Yeah," she said, "But we could start with one or two males, and see how we liked them."

"We've already got pasture," he commented.

I smiled to myself. Deja vu.

9

Llama Packing in the Rockies

"Tie Harlequin over there," Bobra said, "and see if you can catch Spook by yourself." I had sawed off one of Harlequin's fighting teeth the day before, and was glad to see that he bore me no grudge. He followed me placidly. His ears went forward with curiosity as Bobra carried a large green llama pack over to her van.

Spook ran slowly around his pasture, not letting me corner him. I knew that Bobra easily caught her llamas by herself, but Spook seemed to be showing me that he was in control. I decided to show him that I was in control. I didn't really do anything differently, I just told myself that I could catch this llama by myself. Spook stopped by the gate and stood quite still while I put his halter on.

I felt a little uncertain about this pack trip, now that it was about to happen. Was the last time I'd backpacked overnight into the mountains really when I was twelve? I had done a lot of camping and hiking, but with a van as home base. What if it rained? From the ranch you could usually look above Boulder to the jagged skyline of the mountains, but this morning thick clouds obscured the view.

I looked around the ranch. The female herd was just across the fence from me. None of the females had given birth yet. Copper was lying down, a little on her side. Was that an indication? "Hey, Copper, how about it?" I asked her. "Wouldn't you like to have your baby now?" She didn't look at me.

Other people were arriving: there would be nine of us on the trip. Fred and Sonja Anders were llama owners and experienced backpackers. They brought their own llama pack and camping gear, wanting to make this trip a good trial run for trips they would make with their own llamas.

Jan Marts had a few llamas, and had done a lot of backpacking. Her ten-year-old son Kevin was coming too. Carol Smith and Elaine Inglis, both llama owners in the San Francisco Bay Area, had just decided to join us.

Bobra, Margie, and I completed the count. Bobra had been leading llama pack trips for several years. She had taught college before becoming involved with llamas, and it was easy to imagine her steeped in the intricacies of seventeenth century French theater. Margie, her niece, had been my roommate at Bobra's house. She was a young Canadian veterinarian, and if I'd had any stereotypes of what vets were like, Margie had broken them. We'd had a lot of late-night talks about our lives. Margie was to be the cook on this outing, and I had seen enough of her preparations to know that nobody was going to lose weight.

The hubbub of preparations increased as everyone arrived. We loaded the llamas into the van and the trailer, and then piled our belongings in: personal supplies, sleeping bags, tents, llama packs, first aid supplies. There was lots of food for people, but only a little for llamas, as they would graze. The bright blue, green, and red pile of gear reflected contemporary fashions in outdoor equipment. I wondered what a Peruvian llama packer would make of it all, and decided he would probably think it was wonderful.

Copper was standing up, showing no sign of labor. "We'll be back late tomorrow," I told her. "How about having your baby then?"

I rode to the trail head with Jan and her son; she and I talked of how we had gotten into llamas. "I was looking for a small business I could run myself," she said. "I considered several things: running a bookshop, doing consulting, maybe teaching. We already had one llama when it dawned on me that I could get a few more, and turn my hobby into a business."

We arrived at the trail head, a parking lot filled with horse trailers and pickups. We parked next to an empty Rocky Mountain Llamas truck; Bobra's packing partner Steve Eandi had packed in with a group the day before.

We were in the Rockies here, and the clouds were darker
than they had been in Boulder. I felt a drop of rain on
the back of my neck.

As each llama jumped out of the van or trailer, he
looked around with his ears forward. Although I didn't
know these llamas very well, I could see differences in
their personalities. Spook, an elegant black llama and a
veteran of the trail, was completely unspooky.

Handsome was the other old-timer. At home he would
try to fight any other male who came near his pasture,
but here, with no female llamas around, he stood
quietly. I tied him up next to Agate.

"Normally I take no more than one green llama on a
pack trip," Bobra said, "but we're taking three this time.
This is the first pack trip for Harlequin, Nugget and
Agate. They've all had packs on their backs, and they've

*At the trailhead, Nugget sniffs Bobra's hat as she prepares to put
a pack on him. He is wearing the frame developed by Jim Hooks,
useful for carrying unusual loads as well as packs.*

gone on training hikes, but they haven't been out overnight. We have a good combination here--llamas who need packing experience and people who want to learn llama packing techniques!" Several of us in the group had spent the previous day with Bobra at a training clinic, learning such llama esoterica as removing fighting teeth and loading llamas into vans.

Harlequin didn't really seem new to packing. I had walked him around at the ranch, learning how to put a pack on a llama. We'd had a pleasant and uneventful stroll, as if we had been transporting goods together for centuries in the Andes.

Nugget was long, tall, and golden. His coloring showed his part-guanaco heritage; the guanaco is a close relative of the llama, and guanaco-llama crosses are sometimes aloof. Nugget tended in that direction, I thought.

Agate was the smallest of the llamas. His mottled brown and gray markings were very like an agate. He reminded me of my own Tumbleweed, in sweetness and in a similar uncertainty about just what people were up to.

Some of us were putting the saddles on the animals and cinching them with Bobra's guidance. Margie and Carol were weighing every pack bag with a fisherman's scale and marking the weights on pieces of masking tape stuck on the bags.

"That's a good trick," Fred commented.

"It's necessary," Margie explained. "The secret to making the packs stay in place is to have the weight equal on both sides. We're getting them to within half a pound. That's close enough."

I had tied Handsome to the truck when we unloaded. But my newly-learned bowline knot hadn't been quite right, and Handsome's rope was dangling. Nobody else had noticed. I lunged at the rope, before Handsome could decide to go exploring. He gave me a bland look as I tied a perfect bowline.

"Rosana, are you taking Handsome?" Bobra asked.

"Sure, I'd like to. Where are the bags to go on this saddle?"

"Over here," Jan said. She helped me attach them, and Handsome and I were ready to go. Other people and llamas were just starting up the trail.

"Handsome will bring up the rear," Bobra said. "I

often put him at the end. He seems to like it there."

The trail led steeply up into the mountains. As we began a series of steep switchbacks, I felt vaguely anxious. Was it the threat of rain?

"Oh, I'm missing Kelly," I said to myself, relieved to discover what was bothering me. All the wilderness hiking I had done in the past decade had been with him. I missed his quiet presence, his way of enjoying beauty, never too rushed to stop and gaze.

We had been apart for a couple of weeks now. He had intended to come to Boulder with me, but his father's death earlier in the month had changed his plans.

I brought my attention back to the present. It was good to be out and moving after the intensity of the conference. The trail went between spectacular rocks, and the llamas and people ahead of me appeared and disappeared among the boulders. The llamas were brightly laden with packs, the people with daypacks and rain gear. I cheered up and watched the llamas. Handsome and Spook seemed to know that their packs made them wider, but the greener llamas kept bumping the sides of their packs against trees. By the end of the two-day trip, they weren't bumping.

The trail crossed a small stream bed, full of swiftly rushing water. One by one, the llamas crossed, until it was Agate's turn. He just stood by the water. Jan crossed, then tried to coax Agate. He suddenly took a huge flying leap, broad enough to have crossed three streams, and hurried on along the path.

Handsome and I were next. He walked through the water as if it weren't even there.

"Five more stream crossings!" called Margie from ahead of us. "When I scouted out this area last week, I thought they were going on forever." Agate leapt them all; Handsome walked them all.

"Horses ahead!" The word was passed back from the front of the line. We moved off the trail before a party of six or eight horses and riders came by. Horses are sometimes spooked by unfamiliar sights, and llamas are usually unfamiliar. These horses paid little attention to us.

"Seen any other llamas up this way?" asked Carol.

"Yeah, the hills are full of 'em," said an old man on

one of the horses. "Never seen so many in my life."

While we were stopped, I gave Handsome's lead rope to Fred, and went ahead to take some pictures. We were coming out of the steep ravine, and into a more open area of high meadows. Wildflowers and lush grass were waist high in places. From out in the meadow, the llamas looked like they were swimming through the grass.

I walked with Sonja, who was leading Harlequin. Abruptly he sat down in the middle of the trail.

"Hey, fellow, come on, let's get going," Sonja tried to coax him up again. He didn't budge; llamas invented passive resistance centuries ago. I moved around in front of Harlequin and ran at him, waving my arms and yelling "UP! UP!" He stood up.

A few minutes later he went down again. I gave him a repeat performance, and he got right up.

This time Bobra was nearby so I asked her, "Why do you suppose he went down? We checked his pack and it's on him just fine."

"He probably just wanted a rest," she replied. "This is the sort of thing that you may get with a green llama. As they become more experienced, they're less apt to sit down or dash about. I like to let them stand and rest when they've gotten up, then they seldom quit on you."

We stopped for lunch at an open area of old ranches, now part of the national forest. Pioneering must have been rugged here, miles from any town and with severe winters. Those early pioneers could have used some llamas.

We tied out the llamas, but left their packs on. They browsed while Margie laid out breads, cheeses, meats, juices, fruits--food needn't be freeze-dried when the llamas are doing the packing.

Other llamas were grazing in the distance, near a group of tents. We hollered over in that direction, and were greeted by people who had also been at the conference. They told us that the other Rocky Mountain Llamas group was camped a few miles away.

As we hiked after lunch, I watched how the packs sat on the llamas. I wondered which kind of pack would be best for our small males to carry. I pictured Kelly and myself out in the wilderness with a couple of our males carrying packs.

We camped at the edge of another large meadow. There were two very old cabins, one completely littered with broken glass and debris. The other one was usable: the roof was more or less sound, and it had a floor and a front porch. If the windows had ever had glass in them, they didn't any more. The front door was long gone. Rain was still threatening, and the cabin did provide some shelter. We piled our possessions inside.

Bobra had brought several stake pins; they looked like corkscrews for giants. We twisted the pins into the ground, and staked the llamas in a large semicircle around the cabin. They were close enough that people and llamas could keep an eye on each other.

I went for a walk with Elaine. From the upper edge of the meadow, we could see steep snow-covered peaks. Bobra usually packed into much higher elevations, but this year's heavy snow meant that those regions were still inaccessible now, in late June.

A llama bell ringing vigorously sounded like it might mean dinner, and we returned to find that a little village of tents had sprung up around the cabin. As we ate, conversation turned to llama births.

"How many llama babies have been born at your place?" I asked Carol.

"Four so far."

"Have you had any problems?"

"The only problem has been a problem for me, not for the llamas. I haven't seen any of the births yet! The last time, I was determined to see the birth. So I stayed home as much as I could, and tied my pregnant female just outside the back door of my house. I checked her at noon, and everything seemed about the same. Then I took a shower, and when I looked out a few minutes later, she had a baby beside her."

"I think that one of our llamas is pregnant," I said. "I'm hoping for a nice easy birth, and I would love to see one."

"Yes, me too!" Carol said.

After dinner, Margie led a small group off to the other Rocky Mountain Llamas campsite, a mile away.

Those of us who stayed behind led the llamas, two or three at a time, up to a stream to drink. Some would, some wouldn't, but it was pleasant in the long evening twilight, to stroll lazily with a companionable llama.

As we sat on the porch talking, a coyote howled, one long cry, very close. The llamas remained placid. But during the night they were restless--we heard the soft tinkle of their bells. Bobra put bells on her llamas at night so that if one became agitated, she would hear it. The bells made a pleasant sound, which wove itself into my dreams.

"Why were the llamas moving around last night?" I asked in the morning, a steaming cup of tea in my hand.

"Just inexperience, I guess," Bobra said. "It was the green ones who were doing it, I could tell from the sounds of the bells. They may have heard something in the bushes. I looked out of the tent once, and saw Harlequin grazing in the moonlight."

"Oh, wasn't that around the time the revelers came home?" I remembered hearing cheerful voices in the

Fred Anders, Jan Marts, and Bobra attach packs to Agate's saddle.

Spook, Handsome, and Harlequin are loaded up and ready to go. Spook and Handsome have rain covers over their packs.

middle of the night.

Breakfast was another feast. Afterwards, we offered the llamas our orange peels. Harlequin loved them, and ate till he wanted no more. Spook and Agate each nibbled on one, but the others turned their heads away from our outstretched hands.

It was misting lightly. We kept all our rain gear out when we loaded up. Carol pulled out her umbrella.

"That's roughing it," Margie teased.

Our ponchos flapped as we walked, Handsome and I again at the end of the line. Bobra walked with us, and she and I talked of llama books. She was beginning one about training techniques.

We passed a group of hikers with dogs, and just then Harlequin started acting up. He was pulling on his rope and dashing into the trees by the path. Bobra hurried ahead, took his lead rope, and scolded him.

"BAD llama! NO! Now DON"T you do that any more!

Come on, now, settle down, there's a good boy. Come, laddy, yes, that's better." Her voice changed from the tones of a marine sergeant to the murmur of a crooner. Harlequin's walk became smooth again.

"Did the dogs excite him?" I asked.

"No, not at all," Bobra replied. "Everybody's stringing out along the trail, and Nugget got out of sight. I think that's what bothered him. Nugget's his buddy, and he wanted to catch up. Once he could see Nugget again, he was much better."

Leaving the old cabin.

We were making good time along the trail. "Let's stop for a rest and practice tying knots," Bobra suggested. We tied the llamas to trees and bushes. A large bag of trail mix appeared from out of Spook's pack. For a while our hands were occupied with nuts and ropes.

"Llamas ahoy!" came a distant call. Along the trail came the other group. As they passed us, our llamas watched theirs. I was surprised that they showed no signs of excitement, but the llamas did all know each other.

A little later, we caught up with them and made a line ten llamas long. We joined forces for lunch. We were almost at the trail head, so some of the people unloaded the llamas at the vehicles. The rest of us set out the food. The rain was more than a drizzle, and Carol's umbrella became popular; nobody was teasing her now.

With the end of lunch, the pack trip was over. My ride was the first car out, and I had a quiet time at the ranch with the female herd before the other vehicles arrived.

There hadn't been any births yet. Motley was humming a lot; she had been doing that for several days. Copper looked a little larger in the teats, but I wasn't sure. Greyling was doing nothing special. I walked among the llamas, enjoying being with just them. Three-legged Ariel came up and nuzzled me.

The trucks pulled in, and there was a flurry of unpacking and goodbyes. I was staying at Bobra's another day, to help her buy a computer for writing her llama book. We fed the llamas and left, ready for showers and other amenities of urban life.

10

The Birth of Dancing Cloud

I thought eleven and a half months was a long time to wait for anything, but that was how long Posey would be pregnant. Since we didn't know the date of the effective breeding, the waiting period could be over a year from that first Mothers' Day attempt.

I talked with other breeders, and they said that births were generally easy. I asked Parke Duff, a llama breeder who lived near us, if there had been any problem births at his place.

"One morning I came home," he said, "and noticed a tiny head sticking out the rear of one of my females. I went over to see how she was doing. She came up, knocked me down, circled around me, and presented her rump to me. I figured she was asking for help, so I pulled out the baby."

Sometimes I called Sally Taylor for advice, and once I asked her if they had lost many babies. "No, we were fortunate. Our first births were easy, and when we did have some hard ones, we had developed more skill and confidence. It's important to me to be present for the births. I watch my pregnant females very closely and don't even go to the grocery store if I think a female is about to deliver."

Telling when a pregnant female would give birth was tricky. One clue was the size of the expectant mother's teats. Normally tiny, like the tip of a little finger, they would bag up before birth. How soon before seemed to vary from one female to another; it could be several weeks, or just a matter of hours.

When I visited Bobra and Ulo Goldsmith in Colorado, there were three females due any day. Bobra and I looked at one together, and she pointed out that the opening of Copper's vulva was normal in size and shape. When the llama began to dilate, the opening would look longer. It might also look flatter around the vulva as the muscles loosened.

Bobra often helped out during a normal birth, wiping away the mucus from the baby's face and pulling downward on its feet when the mother was pushing. The little ones often started grunting and humming when just the head was sticking out.

I had hoped to see a birth at Bobra's, but as it turned out the first one was forty-five minutes after I left Boulder. I was philosophical; eventually my time would come. Months later, when I was spending a couple of days with Lake and Lawrence Hunter in California, I saw a perfect birth. It took only twenty minutes from the time the hooves appeared until the baby was on the ground.

I had read and re-read the few articles in print about birthing, and I had talked to many breeders. But as the birth began, I abruptly realized how little I knew. As Lawrence pointed out, sometimes the experts contradicted each other about what to do. He and Lake were only a little more experienced than I; two llamas had been born in their herd the previous year, but they hadn't seen the actual births. I was grateful to see this birth before any of our own.

The cria was a female, and therefore worth several thousand dollars more than a male. I was glad for my friends, and I also noticed that the amount of money she was worth brought an increase in tension. The ante had been upped. It was several hours before the new llama began nursing, and it wasn't until she did that I relaxed.

I had thought seeing a birth would be wonderful fun, and partly it was. But it also brought me face to face with my own uncertainties. Midwifery, llama-style, could be scary.

"If Posey would just have as easy a birth," I thought, "that would satisfy me. But I wouldn't mind a girl as well."

Late in April Kelly saw Posey's belly heaving. "The baby must be dancing in there," he reported to me.

I spent hours crawling around in Posey's pasture, trying

to see her teats. Posey watched me, with what I thought was a wondering look, turning so she could watch what I was doing. That made it impossible for me to see her teats. Even when she didn't face me, her wool and the curve of her abdomen made it extraordinarily difficult to see her teats at all. When I did glimpse them, they looked like tiny Hershey's kisses.

Spring and early summer went by. When July came, we knew that it had to be soon. Her last breeding the summer before had been late in July. I had heard that llamas carried their young "eleven to eleven and a half months," and "a year less eighteen days on the average." Then someone told me that first-time mothers often took longer.

Posey was looking bigger in circumference, and her teats were finally enlarged. We moved her into the small llama yard we could watch from the house. She and Lil Bit could still touch noses through a gate, so we didn't think she would be lonely. Kelly said, "Let's review those articles about birth." We quizzed each other on what to do, and made sure that at least one of us was home in the daytime. We knew that most llama babies were born between nine or ten in the morning and four in the afternoon, usually before noon. It was rare for a llama to need help in delivering.

I thought it would be nice if Posey gave birth on my father's birthday, July 11, but she didn't. Friday the 13th came and went without the baby. The following Tuesday, forty-five young children came to see the llamas. She didn't deliver then either.

The next Friday she did seem a little restless. She would sit in one part of her yard, then a few minutes later I would see her in another spot. I looked at her rear, and the vulva was a little longer. But by the time I noticed these changes, it was already past two in the afternoon.

"It'll be tomorrow," I predicted to Kelly. He was finishing an animation project and needed to work in his studio. I had been writing at my computer, and I went back to it, checking Posey every few minutes.

Then I thought, "This is ridiculous. I've been watching Posey so closely for weeks, and now that she's showing new signs, I'm sitting where I can't see her!" I went out to do some gardening near Posey.

It was a warm, sunny day, with a light breeze, much nicer than the heat wave of the previous week. I weeded the lettuce and beets, taking armloads of weeds to different llamas. Then I started in on the asparagus bed. Cider was soaking up the sun in the dusty driveway. Posey was just sitting by the fence, and she wasn't so restless. It was nice to be outside, and the garden certainly needed the work.

I heard a hissing. Kelly had killed a rattlesnake near our house the previous summer, and I immediately thought this was another one. The sound seemed to be coming from the bushes by the driveway, close to Cider and Posey. Both animals had noticed: Posey's ears were back, and Cider picked her head up.

"Just what we need," I grumbled to myself. I grabbed an old piece of barn wood from a stack, looked around me, and cautiously started up the road, prepared to be a heroine. The sound came again--from Posey. I threw aside the board and ran to look at her rear. A hoof was showing.

I ran up the driveway toward Kelly's film studio, calling, "Kelly! Kelly! Feet! Feet!"

A nose and mouth were out and breathing noisily, but I was wrong about the feet. Only one was out. We knew that after some amount of time, if the second one didn't come, someone (me with my smaller hands, probably) would have to scrub up and reach inside Posey to guide the leg out. We didn't know exactly how long to wait before this would become necessary. After five minutes, I ran inside and called our vet's office. Just as I was explaining to the assistant, Kelly called, "Here's the other foot."

"It's okay now, I'll call later to report, bye," I said.

With both feet and the nose out, our biggest fears were gone. Kelly and I hugged and watched. Posey wailed, not a rattlesnake now, just a complaint. All our other llamas were paying attention.

The cria's head, neck, and front legs were out, and they were mostly white. Posey had been sitting down; now she stood up and walked around. She sniffed my tee-shirt, an orange one with an applique flower which she often liked to sniff.

The baby was dangling half-way out of Posey's rear. I suddenly understood the expression llamas breeders use for birth, "hitting the ground." Most llama births occurred with the mother standing, and the baby would indeed hit the ground. But Posey sat down. On the baby's neck. Kelly moved the long neck out from under Posey's back leg, and we put a halter on her in case we needed it.

I put a beach towel under her rear. If we could keep the umbilical cord clean till we put the iodine on, so much the better. I sat down behind Posey.

She was wailing again. The half-born cria was pawing the ground with its front legs. More slippery body emerged, and there it all was. The first llama born at Juniper Ridge Ranch, breathing and wet, mostly white with a few little black spots, and a black tail with a white tip. I savored the moment, without knowing whether the newborn was male or female. I felt very peaceful.

Then I looked. There was a small penis. "It's a boy," I said.

Kelly was busy photographing. "Boy, girl, whatever, isn't it wonderful!" he said.

I flipped the newborn over onto his side. He flailed around as we put iodine on the navel and the end of the umbilical cord, to protect against tetanus and infection. Kelly milked a little out of each of Posey's four teats, just to be sure the milk was flowing. Posey complained with a whine, but let him do it.

The baby sat and rested for a while. Then he stood up, spreading his legs way out for balance. Once up, he stayed in the same position for quite a while. His first steps were wobbly. "Instant toddler," Kelly said.

Kelly watched Posey and the baby while I prepared food for an evening llama hike that was already planned. Luckily I didn't have to think much, as I felt light-headed and my thoughts kept scattering. I did remember to call the vet and report that all was well.

Posey passed the afterbirth. "Don't let her eat it," Howdy had said. "She doesn't need to, and it might upset her stomach." I put it in a bucket, and Kelly gave the cria a selenium injection. Then he weighed himself and the newborn. The bathroom scale was jiggling, but the little one weighed somewhere around twenty-five pounds.

Posey didn't like her baby being handled, and she stayed close by, making clicking noises and threatening to spit. As soon as we were done, we left them alone together, and they sat down for a quiet spell.

The newborn was nursing when people arrived for a hike and picnic supper with Levi and Tumbleweed. I thought of staying with Posey and the baby, but it didn't seem necessary. Kelly checked, and the little fellow was definitely getting milk from all four teats. When we came back from our hike a couple of hours later, he wasn't wobbly on his feet anymore. He was prancing around.

"With that fluffy white wool, he looks like a dancing cloud," Kelly said. "Hey, how about that for a name?"

"Dancing Cloud?" I thought for a minute. "Yes, that suits him."

Our guests left, and we talked while Kelly did the dishes. "What a fantastic mother Posey is," he said. "She hasn't been two feet away from that baby since he was born."

"She's so tender with him," I said. "I love how she keeps sniffing him, and how she steps between him and us, to protect him."

"When he was walking all around her, before he started nursing, did you notice how she stood right where it would be easiest for him to nurse?"

"Yeah. It's interesting that he's mostly white."

"Who'd have thought it? A brown mother, a black father, and a white result. Tell me--are you disappointed that the baby is a male?"

"A little bit," I said. "But it's in a different part of my mind, the budget department or something. How do you feel?"

"Pretty much the same. He's a completely satisfying little creature. It'll be nice if the next baby is a female. When is it due?"

"In six or eight weeks. You know, right now, the way I feel, I'd like a herd of about twenty-five breeding females. I'm not even thinking about the money. It's just such fun."

Kelly smiled. "I'm glad we're living with llamas," he said.

A few minutes after the first glimpse of hoof, the baby's head and feet are out (above left). Posey walks around, the half-born cria dangling behind (left). Most llamas give birth standing, but Posey (above) sits down.

From Posey's open mouth come complaining wails as her baby is born and Rosana reaches to help (left). All the way out and in Rosana's lap (below left), the cria is still wrapped in the amniotic sac. Within minutes, he is rising (below), and his mother gives him a thorough inspection.

With shreds of the amniotic sac on his side, the baby is standing about twenty minutes after birth (above left). His first steps are wobbly, and he leans against his mother (above), guided by instinct to search out her teats. Within an hour, Posey passes the placenta (left). The baby's tail pointing up may mean that he is looking for milk.

Nursing begins (below), and the baby's tail is down. The tail up-tail down signal is not infallible but may indicate whether the youngster is nursing. Posey and Dancing Cloud settle down (right) to sit quietly for a while.

11

Mmmm

"Mmmm," I said to Kelly.

"Mmmm," he replied.

"Mmmm?"

"Mmmm."

We speak llama now. Not, perhaps, with all the nuances of a native speaker, but we are learning all the time. We speak llama, and we have adopted some llama traits. The pre-spitting threat is useful. We blow gently to express curiosity or greeting.

Beyond our acting out, we experience the world differently. We have an additional perspective, the view of the llama. Or, at least, our view of the llamas' view.

When I was nineteen and in Europe for the first time, an old Frenchman told me, "When you are bilingual, then you are twice a person." As I struggled with French, I understood what he meant. There was something about thinking in a different mode that gave me a fresh outlook on life. I haven't used my French in years, but I am again twice a person.

Part II

A Practical Guide

12

On Buying Llamas

Our life with llamas keeps on unfolding. We've bought three more llamas lately, and I could tell you about Romeo and Juliet, and about Poco in the Fourth of July parade. But it's time now for practical information. Part II will cover how and why to buy llamas, care and feeding, training them, packing with them, transporting them, using their wool, and business and financial matters. The last chapter is a resource guide with lots of useful references, names, and addresses.

This book has been read for accuracy by several breeders, and I am content that I am offering you the best overview of llamas that I can. But my years as a reference librarian taught me that even well-researched books can have errors. And knowledge about llamas is increasing all the time.

Kelly and I now do differently some of the activities described in Part I. For example, we didn't quarantine new arrivals, and we were much less thorough about checking into their health than I would probably be now.

For more information on llamas, I particularly recommend the 3L Llama and Speechless Brothers. Llama World is also very good. The Resource Guide has ordering information, and lists other things you may want to read.

WHY LLAMAS?

People buy llamas for packing, breeding, investment, wool, and fun. Llamas have proven utility as packers, whether it's to lighten the load of a vacationer or to carry equipment for a Forest Service crew or a surveyor. Breeding yields babies, and what could be cuter than a baby llama? Becoming a breeder is also an economic decision. As llama prices have risen significantly, the animals--especially the females--have become attractive investments. That was certainly one factor in our decision to buy females. Llamas produce exceptional wool, desirable to hand-spinners, and some people purchase llamas for this reason.

I think that the fun and fascination of having llamas accounts for a great deal of their popularity. We've noticed many times that people find joy in just being around these animals. While they don't offer you the kind of affection a dog does, this has its compensations: if you are away for a while, you don't need to worry about your llamas missing you. They provide fine stress reduction activities; come home from a hard day at the office, and go strolling (or jogging) with your woolly friend. They make good family pets, too. In Bend, Oregon, llamas have been used as 4H projects for several years now. Even very young children can handle llamas with adult supervision. On the llama walks we take at our ranch, preschoolers often lead llamas.

FIRST STEPS

If you think you might want to own llamas, a good first step is finding some to observe. The International Llama Association (ILA), the Llama Association of North America (LANA), and regional groups will supply you with information and names of breeders in your area. Llamas for sale are listed in the classified ads of the 3L Llama, and some breeders advertise in the magazine. Some zoos have llamas; naturally your interaction with the llamas will be more limited than at a ranch, and the llamas' personalities may be somewhat different from ranch-raised llamas.

You may wish to go to a llama conference or get-together. There are a number of regional conferences, in different locations and at different times of year. Many are listed in the 3L Llama. ILA and LANA each have an annual meeting, usually in the summer and usually in the western United States, with many informative speakers. Cost is moderate, and you can talk to lots of llama owners.

Going on a llama pack trip is another good way to become acquainted with llamas. See the chapter on packing, and the list of commercial llama packers in the Resource Guide.

If you live in Canada, one of your first steps should be to look into the Canadian regulations for importing llamas from the U.S. They are quite stringent; you may choose to buy within Canada.

AT LLAMA RANCHES AND AUCTIONS

Go to see more than one herd of llamas. Because llama breeding is a relatively new activity in North America, there is still a lot we don't know. A llama owner may be a sincere and honest person--but not fully informed. By talking with more than one owner, and seeing more than one herd, you'll develop a broader basis for evaluating llamas. Llama owners generally prefer that you telephone for an appointment.

The appearance of a llama ranch may tell you something about the kind of care the animals receive. How secure are the fences? What does the feeding area look like? If it's on the ground and near the llamas' dung piles, there's a greater chance of parasite infestation. Do the llamas have shelter from the extremes of climate?

Notice your personal reactions to the breeders you meet. They have probably heard your questions many times before. Their answers can give you some sense of how helpful they will be to you, if you buy a llama from them. How well do your personalities mesh? If you find yourself all at sea when it comes to recognizing quality in a llama, you may find it useful to draw on your experience of assessing people. After all, you've been doing that all your life.

You may want to ask the breeders how they keep

informed of events in the llama community. Do they belong to any llama organizations? Do they attend conferences? What llama literature do they read?

Ask about prices and sales policies. Breeders often keep waiting lists, especially for females. Some may maintain a list only for special requests, such as a particular color of wool. Some will ask for a deposit, others will not. Some may guarantee a certain price, others won't.

While you are assessing the breeder, he or she may be assessing you. Many breeders are particular about where their llamas go, and they may ask you about your facilities and plans. Selling llamas is a lot more personal than selling computers or refrigerators.

You may be shown animals that are for sale currently, or ones that will be available later. The llamas you buy may be young, perhaps weanlings: youngsters of about six months of age and recently weaned. It is a common practice for breeders to sell unrelated pairs, though some will sell single animals. The breeders may not know exactly when young llamas will be available. But they may be able to tell you something like, "We expect seven babies this fall, and nine in the spring. We sell in pairs. You are sixth on the waiting list, so it's likely to be next spring or the following fall."

Sometimes llama breeders or others act as brokers, either buying and reselling a lot of animals, or acting as a middleman between buyer and seller, perhaps for a percentage of the selling price. Many breeders act as middlemen informally, suggesting that a prospective customer contact another ranch. In some regions the network is well organized.

Zoos sometimes sell their llamas. Because of the "berserk male syndrome"--discussed later in this chapter--you want to find out all you can of the early life of any llama you are considering from a zoo. Since zoo llamas are often hand-raised, I would hesitate to recommend them to a first-time llama owner. Beyond that, the things to look for described for ranches would apply generally to zoos.

Another way to buy llamas is at auction. One annual llama auction is that of Fred Hartman in Tecumseh, Nebraska, late in April. There may be others. Llamas are sometimes sold at exotic animal auctions. I have never attended auctions, but other breeders tell me that auctions can be excellent for educating the eye. You can see many animals gathered together in one place, which does also make it convenient for purchasing.

On the other hand, less information may be available about any particular animal than if you bought it from the breeder. And you have to make decisions in the dramatic atmosphere of the auction. One experienced auction-goer states that the beginning llama owner would be well advised to seek the assistance of someone more experienced.

If you have a friend experienced with llamas, or with other livestock, it wouldn't be a bad idea to take him or her around with you to the ranches you visit as well, especially if you aren't taking a family member or business partner. Then you can compare notes afterward.

SELECTING LLAMAS

Your interests will determine whether you look for juvenile llamas, adult females, or adult males, either intact or gelded (that is, castrated). The evaluation process is generally the same, but in selecting young llamas, keep in mind the advice of breeder Beula Williams. She says, "All babies are cute. Whenever possible, look at the qualities of the sire and dam."

Adult females for sale can be difficult to find. If you are buying an adult female, very likely she is being sold as a bred female. If that is what you are paying for, you may want to have a pregnancy test done. Adult female llamas have a high conception rate after breeding, about 80%, but some of them absorb the fetus early in the pregnancy, or abort, so the test should be recent. People are more likely to sell their less desirable adult females; ask why this particular animal is being sold.

If you are looking for a pack llama and don't plan to become a llama breeder, consider a gelding. Andy Tillman much prefers geldings to intact males for packing, and I'm inclined to agree with him. But this is one of those areas where there are differences of opinion; some experienced llama packers are perfectly happy with intact males. It depends on the situation. If you buy a gelding, and later decide to buy a female, you can breed her to another llama breeder's male, probably paying a stud fee.

Expect to pay quite a lot more for a top-notch trained and experienced packer than for an inexperienced one. If you are eager to start packing, look for an adult male llama.

In selecting any llama, consider its health, conformation, temperament, training, wool, and ancestry. Also notice any intuition you have. I'll discuss each of these topics.

Health

Ask the breeder about the health of the herd in general, and specifically about any animal you are interested in. Has it had any health problems at all? What shots has it had? Did its parents, grandparents or siblings have any health problems? Are any genetic or hereditary abnormalities (minor or serious) known in parents, grandparents, or siblings? (This genealogy may not be known.)

If you're looking at an adult female, what is her birth history? How easy were her births? Has she lost any babies? If you're interested in a juvenile female, ask these questions about her mother.

Find out if the llama has had parasites. Mild cases of internal parasites are common; most breeders test their herds for worms, and give wormers as needed, from one to four times per year, depending on the density of the herd on the pasture, the amount of rain, and other factors. But if a female has had a severe case of worms, she may be a poorer investment.

Examine the animal yourself. Observe if it looks healthy, using the same criteria you would use with any animal: does it seem listless or dull-eyed? Does it show any signs of infection or wounds? Does it have any discharge from nose, eyes, or ears? If you can, touch its body and examine its teeth and feet. As much as possible, feel it all over; most llamas will try to elude you, but do what you can.   To check for lice, part the wool right down to the skin in several places along the spine, and look for tiny moving specks.   Lil Bit had lice recently; what alerted us was that she was scratching along fences and trees so much that she wore off her guard hairs on one side.

You might take the llama's temperature; this can be done rectally with an ordinary human thermometer.   A trick I learned from Bobra Goldsmith is to tie a string to the thermometer, and attach a clothespin to the other end of the string.   Then just pin the clothespin to the wool on the llama's tail, and you'll be sure not to lose the thermometer inside the animal or drop it on the ground.   Andy Tillman says in Speechless Brothers that an adult llama's normal temperature is 100.8 to 101.6 degrees Fahrenheit, and that an infant's is 102.0 degrees Fahrenheit; the form below gives a broader range of values.   If any sizable variation from these temperatures were present, I would ask a veterinarian's opinion.

With all that wool, it can be difficult to judge the fleshiness of a llama.   If you feel the chest of an adult, where it curves down toward the belly, it should be firm--neither bony nor very fat.   Or feel along the backbone; there should be firm flesh around it.   Some breeders look for a well-rounded rump.

Llamas live fifteen to twenty-two years, and the price of an older animal may be less because of its age. Often the exact age of an older llama is not known.

You are within your rights to ask for a veterinary examination (at your expense) as a condition of the sale. It's a very good idea, preferably using a veterinarian who is familiar with llamas.   If you can't find such a person, any veterinarian with livestock experience can look the animal over.

The following is a form developed by Murray E. Fowler, DVM, of the School of Veterinary Medicine at the University of California at Davis. Dr. Fowler is a great friend to llamas and llama owners. He has kindly allowed me to reproduce this form here. It is meant to be used by a veterinarian, but clearly can give you some ideas of what to look for before you consult a vet.

LLAMA HEALTH/SOUNDNESS EXAMINATION

NAME_____ AGE____ SEX: M___ F___ N___
IDENTIFICATION NUMBER_____
SIRE_____ DAM_____
WEIGHT_____ (Actual) or (Estimate)
COLOR_____

VISUAL INSPECTION

BODY CONFORMATION: Fat___, Thin___, Tall___,
    Short___, Balanced___, Straight back, yes___ no___
LIMB CONFORMATION:
    Forelimb (Front view) - Straight___, Curved___
                  (Side view) - Straight___, Bent___
    Hindlimb (Hind view) - Straight___, Curved___
                  (Side view) - Straight___, Bent___
COMMENT:
WOOL COAT: Uniform___, Patchy loss___, Length_____
    Foreign matter (burrs, awns)___, Crusts, sores___
GAIT: Moves freely_____, Lameness_____
FECAL PELLETS: Normal, yes___ no___

CLOSE INSPECTION

TEMPERATURE_____ (Normal 99-102.5 F.)
HEAD AND NECK
LIPS: All movements normal_____, Swelling_____
    Drooling saliva or feed_____
TEETH: Lower jaw too long_____, Broken teeth_____
    Missing teeth_____, Gums normal, yes___, no_____
    Status of canines_____.
EYES: Pupils responsive_____, Lids normal_____
    Cornea clear, yes___ no___; Cataract, yes___ no___
    Responsive to visual stimulation, yes___ no___
EARS: Movements okay, yes___ no___,
    Discharge, yes___ no___
SKIN: Scars, yes___ no___, Enlargements, yes___ no___
BODY
HEART: Heart rate (Normal is 60-99/minute)
    Resting_____, Excited_____
    Murmur, yes___, no___; Arrhythmic, yes___ no___
LUNGS: Respiratory rate (Normal is 10-30/minute)

Resting_____, Excited _____
Sounds normal, yes___ no___
ABDOMEN: Stomach motility (Normal averages 4/minute,
   but may have 5-8 one minute and none the next)
   Actual_____, Umbilical hernia, yes___ no___
SKIN: Areas of wool loss, yes___ no___
   Dermatitis, yes___ no___
FEEL MUSCLE MASS over ribs, back, and pelvis.
LIMBS
LEFT FORE: Visual OK, yes___ no___
   Palpation OK, yes___ no___
   Nail OK, yes___ no___
   Pad OK, yes___ no___
LEFT HIND: Visual OK, yes___ no___
   Palpation OK, yes___ no___
   Nail OK, yes___ no___
   Pad OK, yes___ no___
RIGHT HIND: Visual OK, yes___ no___
   Palpation OK, yes___ no___
   Nail OK, yes___ no___
   Pad OK, yes___ no___
RIGHT FORE: Visual OK, yes___ no___
   Palpation OK, yes___ no___
   Nail OK, yes___ no___
   Pad OK, yes___ no___
SCALY OR CRUSTY AREAS, yes___ no___
MANGE MITES (SARCOPTIC), yes___ no___
COMMENTS:
GENITAL ORGANS
FEMALE: Vulva normal yes___ no___
   Discharge yes___ no___
MALE: Testicles in scrotum yes___ no___
   Penis normal yes___ no___
GENERAL COMMENTS:

On the basis of visual inspection and physical
examination, I find this animal to be healthy.
NAME: DVM (signature)
                                    (print)

ADDRESS:

TELEPHONE:(   )   DATE:

Conformation

Conformation is a word used by animal fanciers to describe how an animal conforms to certain criteria for appearance. Although there are no official standards for what a llama should look like, conformation is still a useful concept. If you haven't examined livestock or dogs with an eye for conformation, you may well find this to be confusing at first. Just keep looking at llamas, and your taste will develop. There is plenty of room for individual differences.

A straight topline along the back is admired by many breeders, though it's not always easy to tell under the wool. Some breeders think that substantial bone is better than a more delicate look. Relatively straight legs are more popular than knock knees, but keep in mind that a slight bow to the legs is quite normal. They are usually not perfectly ruler straight. Tumbleweed has a bit of a knock-kneed look, so we will keep that in mind when choosing what females to breed him to. But it certainly didn't stop us from buying him, when he had several traits we wanted.

Ears are important to some: I've known a breeder to turn down a particular llama because of its ears. Many llamas have banana ears, curving inward in a banana-like shape. The ear length can vary. A few llamas have ears that are bent at the tips. Some breeders don't like tipped ears, but others like them fine. I think they can be charming. Tipped ears can be inherited, or caused by extremely cold conditions when the llama was young.

As in choosing your human companions, looks aren't everything. Buy what you like and think you'll enjoy looking at. If you do intend to breed, you may not find your ideal immediately. Part of the fun of breeding is working toward it.

Temperament

Llamas are often typified as calm and intelligent, and most llamas are. Each one has its own distinctive personality. We don't know yet to what extent disposition is inherited and how much it's a result of experience.

Woolly ears, tipped ears, and banana ears. (All photos by Susan L. Jones)

Clearly, both are operative.

Especially if you intend to form a close relationship with your llamas, spend some time observing the ones you are considering. Ask about their temperaments. Have they suffered any emotional trauma the breeder knows about? I forgot to ask this about Posey, and nobody thought to mention her fear of dogs, so I didn't learn of it until she was at our place. No harm was done in that case, but I will ask in the future.

If you are purchasing males, ask how much they were handled during their first six months of life. The "berserk male syndrome" can occur in males who have been handled incorrectly or too much during those early months. There may be other causes as well. Some breeders feel that "berserk" is too strong a word, but the trait itself is well documented.

Basically, if an infant male spends a lot of time with people, he will think that people should be treated like llamas. Normal adult male llamas threaten and attack each other. Therefore, he may threaten and attack people. It's all very logical from his point of view, but potentially dangerous to people.

Bottle-fed babies can be quite delightful, but bottle-fed males must be castrated between three and six months to avoid the risk of 'berserk male syndrome.' No llama baby should be bottle fed unless necessary, and it should be raised as much among llamas as possible. (Susan L. Jones)

If a young male has had to be bottle-raised or otherwise handled a lot, it's advisable to castrate him at three to six months of age, prior to selling him. This is generally believed to eliminate the chance of "berserk" behavior. Llama owners are in disagreement about how much a young male can be handled without requiring castration. Some say that a llama can be worked with when young, so long as it is properly disciplined, but until more is known I prefer to handle the youngsters very little, deferring training until after weaning at five or six months. In Peru, llama-owning parents teach their children not to make pets of the young intact males.

I had one experience of a "berserk" sort, and I found it unnerving. With his owner, who had recently acquired him from another part of the country, I entered the pasture of a large, adult male. The llama came running across the field. I was used to that, as our llamas often do the same, stopping just a few feet away. This llama kept coming, and hit me in the head with his neck. I was astonished. Then I jumped the fence.

A female who has been handled a lot when young may be overly friendly, pesky, or difficult as an adult, but she isn't likely to hurt you. By nature she has less inclination to challenge others than does a hand-raised male.

Training

You want to know what a llama you are going to buy can do. Is it halter broken? Does it follow if on lead? Will it jump into a vehicle or trailer? How much will it allow you to touch it, on various parts of its body? If you are interested in hiking and packing, has it had any training in these areas?

If you are buying weanlings, their training may not have started or may be very limited. There is rarely a price difference in adult females because of training, but for adult males there is. Sellers are sometimes optimistic about how well trained a llama is.

Wool

If you are a spinner or weaver, or if you intend to sell llama wool, it is a factor in selecting an animal. If you are trying to obtain a particular color, ask the breeder to show you a sample of the llama's wool. Lil Bit looks primarily brown, but her undercoat, which is mainly what combs out, is gray. Other things to look for include length of wool, and the amount of guard hair. See the chapter on wool for more details.

If you are looking for a male to use for packing, keep in mind that the white and light-colored llamas don't get as hot as the dark ones. We have found that Levi, who has coarse and plentiful guard hairs, stays much cleaner than some of our llamas with fewer and finer guard hairs.

Ancestry

You may be able to find out something about a llama's ancestry, but in most cases the records will not go back many generations. What you are told may be inaccurate. This situation is changing; breeders are keeping better records all the time.

You may come across llama-guanaco crosses. The guanaco is a close relative of the llama, and the two can interbreed. While llamas have been domesticated for thousands of years, there are still herds of wild guanacos. Bill Franklin, an expert on guanacos, says, "Guanacos generally have a more independent disposition than llamas, but when they are raised in captivity, they can be equally pleasant. They are just as tamable." Guanaco wool is not as long as llama wool, but it is finer. In South America and Europe, guanaco wool is a multi-million dollar industry; Bill told me of men's coats woven from it that sold for $3000 to $5000.

Pure guanacos are a golden reddish-brown on the upper body, with a darker brown to black tail. The belly and neck are white, and the face is gray to black. Guanaco-llama crosses may inherit some or all of this coloring, but they won't necessarily.

The crosses are, of course, neither llama nor guanaco.

This mother is believed to be pure guanaco, while her baby is a llama-guanaco cross. Their ears are more pointed than is typical of the llama. (Susan L. Jones)

Some llama breeders don't like the crosses, while others do. I have known a couple of llama-guanaco crosses who were fine pack animals. The main point for a beginner is simply to be aware that the crosses exist, and to make your choices based on what appeals to you. The crosses sometimes, but not always, sell for less than llamas.

A number of llama-alpaca crosses were among the camelids brought in from Chile in 1983 and 1984. I haven't seen any of them yet.

Your Intuition

Take time to notice your sense of the animal. Your intuition may not be saying anything, but then again, you may experience a feeling of uncertainty or a sense of rightness. I have found intuition to be a valuable adjunct to the rational mind in making business (or any) decisions.   When I hesitated to buy Lil Bit, as discussed in Part I, I was allowing room for my intuition to be heard.

THINKING IT OVER

After visiting breeders, think it all over.   Are llamas for you?   Do you have the time, the space, and the desire?   Llamas don't have to take much time, but the more you enjoy them, the more you'll want to be out with them.   That time will have to come from somewhere.

If necessary, they can go a few days on a big pile of hay and plenty of water, but normally somebody needs to feed and inspect them daily.   Fixing fences, training the llamas, and so on, does take time.   If you want to go away, you need to find a llama-sitter, or at least a neighbor to stop by.

As for space, it is good to have an acre or more.   But llamas have been kept in large urban backyards.   If you intend to do that, you might want to see if your city allows it.   If you don't have a fenced pasture, you can rent one in many suburban and rural areas.   Quite a few llama owners are city dwellers who enjoy weekend visits with their llamas in the country.

How strong is your desire for llamas?   Do you want them enough to willingly face the prospect of going out to feed in the pouring rain before leaving for work at 7:30AM?   How would you feel about delaying the family vacation because your female hadn't given birth yet?   What are your reasons for wanting llamas?

I've suggested that you ask a lot of questions, but I haven't told you how to deal with all the possible answers.   For example, if a female has had two babies and lost one, you might still want to buy her.   At least you'll know her track record.

Some people are more casual about what llamas they buy than Kelly and I have been.   Others are more particular.   I believe it's well worth your time and effort to be thorough, especially if you may do some breeding. A better llama is a better investment.

People do buy llamas sight unseen. We almost did, but we decided ultimately that we just weren't sure enough. A breeder I know did it once, and the animal was so ugly to his eyes (despite nice photos) that he promptly sold it at a loss. I think I might buy a llama sight unseen if it was highly recommended by another breeder whose taste in llamas I knew and trusted, if my intuition was strongly favorable, and if the llama was thoroughly examined by a veterinarian. Even then, I would certainly prefer to go see the animal.

You may be inclined to start out with just one llama. We were going to, but we are very glad we didn't. Llamas are so very social that it seems a pity to take them entirely away from their own kind. Two llamas cost more than one, it's true. But if that's a problem, perhaps you can buy one and some friends buy another. You could keep them together. Or you might buy one, and board it at another llama owner's.

If you want to buy just one, arrange to spend a few hours watching a llama herd. Observe the subtleties of the interactions. Then see if you still have the heart for separating a llama from its kind. If you do, seriously consider a gelding, or castrated male. They seem to adjust better to bachelorhood, without the powerful sex drive of an intact male. Single llamas do need other four-legged companionship, be it dog, goat, horse, or whatever. If completely alone, it will be unhappy.

PRICES AND PAYMENT

At this writing, male llamas sell for $1000 and up, and females, $6500 or more. Outstanding animals with bloodlines considered desirable may sell for much higher sums. In 1982, when we bought our first llamas, males began at $500 and females at $4000. What will prices be when you are reading this? Probably higher. We are beginning to see more of a range of prices, depending on the owners' assessment of the quality of the animals.

Expect to pay the breeder in full for the llamas; it isn't customary for breeders to offer terms. Ask for a receipt. Depending on the circumstances, payment may be asked for at the time you choose a llama, or perhaps partly then and the remainder when you pick up the animal. A small deposit may be required just to be on a waiting list. Sometimes people request babies before they are born, based on the qualities of the parents. Whatever the arrangement, be clear whether any deposits are refundable and if so under what conditions, and at what time ownership of the animal passes to you.

BEFORE THEY COME

Before your llamas arrive, arrange a fenced area. Purchase some hay, loose mineralized salt, and a water container. Devise a shelter. Locate a veterinarian in your area, preferably one who has worked with llamas, and ask him or her about local problems: selenium levels in the soil, rabies in the area, etc. If the breeder isn't supplying them, obtain one or two llama halters and lead ropes.

If you haven't already done so, ask the breeder to write out as much of your animal's parentage as is known. In many cases, it may be only the parents. Or possibly not even them. But any information will be interesting and helpful. It could keep you from buying related llamas from different breeders without realizing the connection. Take color photos of the parents if possible; if not, perhaps the breeder has some to give you. Ask if the animal is listed with the Camelid Identification System of the International Llama Association or if it's on the list of the Llama Association of North America.

Have the breeder give you your llama's health record. What has it been wormed with? What inoculations has it had, and when is it due for the next ones? Also ask the breeder if you can buy several days' hay, so that the llama can adjust to new hay gradually. If you don't know how to halter your llamas, ask the seller to show you how.

You may bring the llamas home yourself, the breeder might bring them, or you might hire a commercial llama trucker. If you're transporting the animals across state lines, a veterinary certificate of health and certain specialized tests may be required; call the state department of animal control, or if there isn't one, your county agent can probably tell you who to contact. Tests might be required for brucellosis, blue tongue, anaplasmosis, tuberculosis, or other diseases.

If you already have other llamas, isolate the newcomers for two or three weeks, preferably keeping them at least twenty to thirty feet away from your herd. When feeding during this quarantine time, it's advisable to handle the newcomers after the others, so that if the new llamas do have a health problem, you won't act as carrier. We like to have our veterinarian look over new llamas during the first week or two.

As you go through the process of looking for and buying llamas, take the time to enjoy it. One way or another, you'll find your llamas. And then the fun really begins.

13

Care and Feeding

Llamas are easy to care for. Give them good hay, fresh water, salt, and a mineral supplement; fence their pasture or yard; give them a simple shelter, offering protection from sun, rain and snow; inoculate them annually; worm them at least once a year; have a veterinarian you can call if you need to.

Like many simple things, there's a lot more that can be said. I'm going to say enough to give you a good start.

FOOD AND DRINK

Llamas are browsers, which means they will nibble on many different kinds of plants. If you have pasture for them, they will gladly eat pretty much anything in it. This includes trees: wrap trunks with chicken wire or surround them with stakes. After you have had the llamas a while, you may notice an area of lush grass which they don't eat. That will be around a dung pile. They avoid such places, a habit which serves to keep down the incidence of parasites. Some people steep llama manure in water and pour the resulting 'tea' on trees they don't wish the llamas to eat. Naturally, this works best in areas of little rainfall.

Some breeders may have enough pasture to feed their llamas on it year-round, but for most, seasonal supplementation with hay and perhaps grain is required. If llamas are kept in a small space, or in an area of poor soil, hay may need to be their major food source year round.

We feed some alfalfa and some grass hay, in about a fifty-fifty mixture.   Oat hay may be fed instead of grass hay.   Many llama owners feed alfalfa hay only, but some experts believe that it provides more protein than the llamas need.   In addition, a diet of only alfalfa may be conducive to ulcers and other health problems.   When we tried our llamas on straight alfalfa hay, their urine smelled very strong.   As soon as we mixed that hay with grass hay, the smell became much milder.

The price of hay varies according to protein content, location, weather, how it has been stored, and whim.   We

A slatted hay holder at Oregon Llamas.

have found up to a 35% variation in prices when phoning around, with the most expensive hay not necessarily the best. Classified ads and the yellow pages under "Hay" or "Feed" should give you some leads.

Hay is sold by the bale or by the ton. Bales can weigh anywhere from 50 to 120 pounds, so if you are quoted a per-bale price, ask what the average weight is, to compare costs. In choosing hay, check that it has little or no mildew or mold. Mildewed hay isn't worth feeding, as it could have allergic or other bad effects. Alfalfa hay should be bright green, a sign that it still has plenty of vitamin A in it.

If the hay is extremely low in nutritional value, it may be physically impossible for a llama to consume enough of it. It's a good idea to have hay tested for TDN (total digestible nutrition) or to get a report from the grower or feed dealer.

A llama consumes between 2% and 4% of its body weight in food per day. If the llama is being used for packing, is in the last month of pregnancy, or is nursing, then more is needed. Growing babies also need more

Llamas are very interested in food. (Susan L. Jones)

after weaning. In these cases, feeding conditioners developed for other livestock or some grain will ensure that the animal gets enough protein. Grain refers to bran, oats, corn or barley, either plain or sweetened with molasses. It is possible for llamas to overeat, especially if given too much grain. Be sure they can't get into where you keep your grain. We call the sweet version "llama granola" and use it primarily for treats.

If you don't know how much your adult llamas weigh, you can judge their condition by feeling the front of the chest, just above the front legs. You should be able to feel some fat there, but not a great deal. Or feel along the spine. If you check your animals from time to time, you'll come to know what's normal for them.

Generally, llama owners tend to err on the side of giving too much feed, with the result that some llamas are too fat. Sheron Herriges, an expert on birthing and care of newborns, says that many of the calls she receives are from people with overweight mother llamas.

Llamas need minerals, and these can be given in the form of mineral salts, loose or in a block. We found that ours ignored the block, so we fed loose salts. We weren't sure that they were getting enough even then, so we switched to a pelletized vitamin and mineral supplement we mix in with a little grain. In areas where selenium is deficient (and this includes much but not all of the western United States), it should be included. In some parts of the country, there is too much selenium in the soil. Ask your veterinarian or county extension agent about your region.

Water should be fresh daily, and always available. When llamas are out packing, they often go two or three days before drinking, so they are quite hardy in this respect. They drink surprisingly little, generally less than a gallon a day in cold weather. But it's important that they have it when they want it, especially nursing mothers and all llamas in hot weather. They will drink more then.

There are plants that llamas should not eat. Any plant known to be poisonous to livestock or to people should be avoided. Some common house and yard plants to beware of include daffodils and other common bulbs (the bulbs), oleander, diffenbachia, ivy, poinsettia, mistletoe (the berries), rhododendron, and azaleas. There are more. Outside, there are many; see the Resource Guide for a list. Luckily, llamas like to nibble on a little of this and some of that, so it is only the most lethal plants that are likely to cause problems. Poisonous plants could be included in hay you buy; ask the seller if there is any chance of it containing tansy ragwort. If the answer is yes, don't buy it.

Most (though not all) poisonings will occur rather quickly, so if you do suspect that a llama may have been poisoned, call your veterinarian immediately! Prompt care can make a big difference.

You may notice llamas sitting and chewing their cuds. The llama is called a modified ruminant, because the different chambers of its stomach are less separated than in other ruminants such as cattle.

LIVING ARRANGEMENTS

Land and Fencing

Because conditions vary so widely, it is hard to say how much land llamas need. One rule of thumb is four adult llamas or six weanlings per acre of good quality pasture, with supplementary feed given as needed. I know of excellent llama ranches more populated than this, but on our sparse soil the ideal would be fewer animals per acre.

It's desirable to be able to rotate pastures, both to reduce parasites and to allow the pasture time to renew itself. I like Sally Taylor's recommendation of two or three pastures more than you think you need.

Depending on the number, ages, and sexes of the animals you have, it's useful to have a series of interconnecting pens and gates, so you can move the llamas around as you wish. Because llamas are so social, try to position things so that any llama kept alone can see others. A small pen or corral, sometimes called a "catch pen" is handy not only for catching but also for combing, handling, training, and just being with llamas.

If you have a lot of unfenced land, as we do, or when

*Good pasture is desirable, though not essential, for llamas.
(Susan L. Jones)*

you are out camping, llamas may be staked out. Stake
pins that screw into the soil are available, but our soil is
too loose. We tie the llamas to rocks, trees, shrubs,
whatever is handy, so long as they can't become seriously
entangled in it. Sometimes we use large logs. We used
cinder blocks until Levi ran a quarter of a mile, pulling
one behind him, when I had taken Tumbleweed for a walk
without him. We never leave llamas staked out when
nobody is home.

Llama breeders use a variety of kinds of fencing.
Simple wooden fences and woven wire are popular.
Electric fence is inexpensive; some breeders have found it
useful, others have been unhappy with it. New Zealand
fencing is also used. Barbed wire is generally avoided.
Llamas don't need it, as they aren't hard on fences, and
the barbs can scratch them.

Llamas don't tend to be fence-jumpers, though I've
heard of a male llama jumping a six-foot fence to breed
a female. Many breeders use four foot fencing.

Kelly and I prefer six-foot woven wire for the main
llama areas. That's partly because the snow drifts up to
seven or eight feet where the llamas are, but it's also to

keep dogs out. We have heard too many accounts of
dogs getting in and running young llamas so severely that
the youngsters had to be put down. Adult llamas can
take better care of themselves with dogs, but it still can
be a concern.

Shelter

Llamas need a place to go in from the rain or snow,
though they may not use it. On one farm where the
winter temperatures were often twenty below zero,
several llamas chose to sleep outdoors one winter rather
than share a shelter with a cow. They did fine--and
their owners did give them separate quarters later.

Llamas will be perfectly content with even very simple
shelters. Three-sided sheds are often used, with the open
side not facing toward the prevailing wind. If you are
planning to breed, a stall where the newborn and mother
can be kept cozy and quiet is desirable.

As llamas don't like dark places in the daytime,
corrugated fiberglass roofing, either clear or translucent,
may be used as all or part of a roof. We use it for
about one-fourth of our roofing, because it doesn't take
the snow load well.

Shade in hot weather is important, and may be
provided by the shed or by trees. Also in hot weather,
flies may become a problem. A "Big Stinky" type
collecting container can be used for flies, and there are
other methods of fly control, IPM (Integrated Pest
Management) as well as pesticides. See the Resource
Guide for more about IPM. In heat waves or other
extremely hot weather, some llama owners provide
sprinklers, children's plastic wading pools, or other cooling
devices. The llamas seem to enjoy standing in the
sprinklers.

If the flies are coming from the manure piles, putting
straw down or removing the manure helps. I use a lot of
manure in our gardens, though I don't put it in direct
contact with plants I'm going to eat (like carrots) until it
has aged a season. Llama manure is so good for gardens,
that some llama owners--finding themselves with an
abundance of the stuff--have sold it to gardeners.

Security

While theft of llamas is rare, it does happen. Preventative measures you can take include good fencing, keeping your llamas in a safe location, checking them regularly, not telling callers when you will be away, guard dogs, and the like. Several breeds of dog used in Europe for centuries as guard dogs are being researched in the U.S. as livestock guardians. Great Pyrenees, Komondor, and lesser-known breeds are being used.

"Our llamas had been attacked by a pack of dogs from a nearby subdivision," Steve Rolfing told me. "After we got a Great Pyrenees, there were no more problems. She's run off some bears too. We raised her with two weanling llamas, and she's both playful and protective with them. We trust her completely with our animals and with our young daughter."

Dogs are the greatest four-legged hazard to llamas; coyotes are rarely, if ever, a problem. Some llama owners feel that llamas pastured with sheep might chase any coyotes trying to prey on the sheep. While llamas have been sold for this purpose, and some research has been done, I don't know if the llamas' utility in a working situation has been confirmed.

If a llama should be stolen, good color photographs--from both sides, front, and rear--will increase the likelihood of your being able to claim the animal if it turns up. Ear tattooing is being explored, particularly by LANA.

HEALTH CARE

Llamas tend to be healthy, and there are a few simple things you can do to help them stay that way. Worming is one of them. We take a little plastic bag of llama pellets in to our veterinarian every four months. He checks for internal parasites. If they are present (and they sometimes have been), he gives the llamas one of several different worming medications that are on the market.   We rotate wormers, as do many llama owners, to keep the parasites from becoming resistant to any one.   Ivermectin, a newly available wormer, is effective against many internal and external parasites.   The bovine form is used for llamas.   No drugs have been approved for llamas as such.

Our llamas are inoculated annually against tetanus, clostridial diseases, and leptospirosis.   Because soil in our region is deficient in selenium, we also give an annual injection of a selenium supplement.   We worked out our inoculation program with our veterinarian.   Some llama owners choose not to inoculate, partly because the vaccines were developed for other animals.   Whether you vaccinate may also depend on the amount of contact your llamas have with other animals.

Many llama owners do their own worming and inoculating.   We may eventually ourselves, but our vet's farm call is a good excuse to visit with him.   Each time he comes, we learn a little more about what to do--and I think he learns a little more about llamas.

Find a veterinarian for your llamas before you need one.   If you already have a vet, ask if he or she is interested, or can recommend someone.   If you know other llama owners in your area, ask them whom they use.   Veterinarians who are new to llamas would probably like to know about the ILA veterinary workshops, telephone Hot Line, and other sources of information.

Some llamas need their toenails trimmed.   Of our herd, only two do.   We use heavy-duty shears; toe snippers will also do the job.   It isn't difficult, particularly if you accustom the llama to having its legs handled.

Removing fighting teeth of males is recommended. Some llama owners restrain a male llama and saw the tooth off with veterinary obstetrical wire.   Others prefer to make more of a surgical procedure of it, having a veterinarian anesthetize the animal and remove more of the tooth.

Summertime brings with it the danger of heat stroke if you are keeping llamas in a very hot place.   Providing water and shade is essential, but if you find yourself with a prostrate llama, hose it down and call the vet.   The wool actually insulates llamas from the heat, so don't shear them with the idea of cooling them off.

Flies can be pesky in warm weather, and we sometimes put a little human or horse insect repellent on a llama's head.   Other hazards of warmer weather include ticks and rattlesnakes.   Like humans and dogs, llamas are subject to tick paralysis.   In one instance a llama was given a close shearing in order to find the ticks.   Two were removed, and the llama soon recovered.   Rattlesnakes can kill llamas, and this has happened.   Llamas have to breathe through their noses.   Since most snake bites in llamas occur on the nose, a piece of tubing (small hose) placed in the nostril before swelling occurs may save the animal's life.   In any case of suspected snake bite, get the help of a veterinarian immediately.

If this catalog of health care is enough to make you give up the idea of llamas (and of course there are plenty of rare problems I haven't even touched on), do think again.   Generally, llamas are healthy and easy to have around.   They live an average of 15 to 22 years, and really are quite hardy.

BREEDING AND BIRTHING

In choosing a male to breed to your female, be sure that they are unrelated or only distantly related.   It's good if the female's weak points can be balanced by the male's strong points; for example, a female with little wool or delicate bone would ideally be bred to a male with abundant wool and sturdier bone.   This depends, of course, on what you like in llamas.   If you don't have a male to complement your female, you might take her to another ranch or farm for breeding.   Stud fees are generally reasonable.   The stud's owner may request that you have a veterinary certificate of health for your female.   You can't really ask the same of his whole herd, but do be selective about where you take an animal.

Some breeders keep track of when they breed, putting the male and female together and then separating them. This gives you the best idea of when to expect the baby, and is widely done by owners of small herds.   Other breeders are more apt to keep a male in with a number of females all the time.   Once a female is pregnant, she won't usually permit a male to mount her. This system has the advantage that if the female spontaneously aborts, she'll soon let the male breed her.

Pregnancy tests have become available recently, and are modest in price. You send a blood sample to a lab, and the amount of progesterone in the system indicates whether the female is pregnant. You can learn if your female has settled by doing this test about three weeks after breeding (we do it at around twenty-five days), and it's advisable to do it again two or three months later to make sure she remains pregnant. Re-absorbing the fetus is fairly common, and you may need to breed her again. Serious fertility problems in female llamas are rather rare, and as you can imagine, a topic of interest to breeders. We are learning more as the llama industry becomes larger and better organized.

Birth is about eleven and a half months after breeding, almost always during the daylight hours, and usually in the morning. Around ninety-five percent of all births are normal, calling for little or no human assistance. If assistance is needed, you would most likely have to reposition the cria's limbs while it is still in the mother.

You will want to have a kit of supplies on hand before a birth. Different people have different things in their kits; ours contains surgical tape to tie off the umbilical cord if necessary (dental floss is often used); seven per cent iodine to put on the navel and tip of the unbilical cord; a lubricant called J-lube, and one called Septi-Lube, for use if we need to reach inside the mother; surgical scrub for washing hands and arms; a clean pair of scissors; an ear syringe meant for humans, to suck away any mucus around the baby's nose; and an enema bag, to give the cria a plain water enema if it doesn't have a stool in the first few hours. Our veterinarian gave us a selenium mixture (1 ml. Bo-Se) and the needle to inject it into the newborn (under the skin and easy to do), but the need for this would depend on the region.

We also have a clean bottle with a nipple in case the cria doesn't start nursing quickly. If we had to milk the mother, we could give that first milk to the baby. It's called colostrum, and full of antibodies and other good things for the baby. It's a good idea to have some colostrum in the freezer in one ounce chunks; llamas' is best, but goat or calf is better than nothing.

Copies of the articles about birthing listed in the Resource Guide, several large towels, a heat lamp, a place to separate the mother and cria from the rest of the herd, and a card with the phone numbers of our vet and several experienced llama breeders complete our arrangements.

In the first hours after a birth, you have to make sure the placenta is passed and that the cria is nursing and getting milk. Watch it closely for the first few weeks of life. You'll probably be gazing at it all the time, but take time from admiring its delights to generally look it over for condition. You can rebreed the mother two or two and a half weeks after delivery.

KEEPING RECORDS

A record for each llama will be useful, for yourself and anyone who buys a llama from you. The record we keep for each animal lists its name; sex; date of birth; our identification number; the CIS (Camelid Identification System) number of the llama; how we acquired it; date acquired; price paid; from whom we acquired it; a description of the animal and of its wool; height at withers; weight (and whether estimate or weighed); a detailed health record including all injections and medications; the name and description of its mother, father, and their parentage, as far back as is known; training; breeding; to whom sold; date sold; price sold for; date and cause of death; and general remarks We also keep color photos of each animal, and where possible, of its parents. I wouldn't say that we are always caught up on our computer, but we do at least toss a scribbled note in a shoebox whenever a veterinary procedure is done. Computers can be wonderful, but shoeboxes are here to stay as well. However you keep records, the llama community will benefit from the increased knowledge.

14
Training, Packing, and Transport

TRAINING

The more you train your llamas, the more fun you will have with them. If you have ever trained any animal, you may be surprised at how easy it is to work with llamas. If you're new to animal training, you're entering a fascinating field. When we began with llamas, the extent of my background was one six-week dog obedience class with Cider. I've been delighted with how quickly the llamas learn. And with how quickly I learned.

They need almost no rote training. Andy Tillman comments in Speechless Brothers, "Though I grew up with horses and mules, I would put my trust in a [male] llama with only one week's training more than I would in a gelding horse with several seasons of trail experience. Considering that horses have two years of fairly frequent training before ever setting foot on a trail, that's saying something." Andy pointed out to me in conversation that if we rode llamas, they would need more than a week's training, but the point remains that llamas are calmer and far more easily trained than horses.

Bobra Goldsmith coined the rule of four: usually, the fourth time you show a llama what you want it to do, it really catches on. The only time you will have to go over and over something is if you are correcting an old habit. For example, we made several mistakes in trying to halter-break Levi and Tumbleweed, and they drew the conclusion that halters were unpleasant. It took maybe twenty halterings after that before they were easy to halter.

We like to teach all our llamas to be catchable, to accept the halter, to lead easily, and to let themselves be handled. Our males are taught to carry a pack, and usually to load into a trailer or vehicle. Many llama owners teach their llamas to sit down on command; while this can be useful, we haven't found it to be as essential as the first four elements.

People with larger herds often do less training of their animals. Especially if there are several strong people around the place, they can restrain any animal as needed.

It's handy to be able to catch a llama easily. Bobra Goldsmith explained to me that there often develops a ritual or pattern in catching a llama. Whiskers typifies it: when I walk into his yard, he runs around a little. I wait, or perhaps walk toward him. In a minute or less, he walks to the gate, ready for his halter. Catching is less a matter of training than it is of adapting yourself to the animal and developing a habit in the llama. It's easier in a small space (often called a catch-pen) than in a large field.

Spending quiet time with a llama before catching may reassure it if it is nervous. Move slowly, especially right at the end when you are about to put your arms, and a rope, around the llama's neck. The tendency is to rush at this point, but the llama will stay calmer if you move slowly. I am not above the bribe of a snack to lure a llama close to me, but llamas are so smart they know what I'm up to, and the bribe only works if they are willing to be caught. I use snacks more as reward for good performance.

Once you can catch the llama, haltering is the next step. When we first haltered Posey and Lil Bit, we didn't realize they were learning to be haltered just by our doing it. Soon we noticed that if we put the halter an inch or two in the air in front of their noses, they pushed forward into it.

When you introduce the halter, let the llama smell it. Stand on his left side. Some people find their llamas are more approachable from one side than the other; whether this is a human expectation or a llama trait, I don't know. If your llama would much prefer to be approached from the right, do that. I only suggest the left because the halters are designed to be fastened on the left. Reach your right arm around his neck, hold the halter open in both hands, and ever so slowly bring it onto his face. He may try to elude you by moving his neck around; if so, follow his nose as closely as you can with the halter. You may want to do this a number of times before fastening the halter. Once that's done, clip a lead rope onto the ring at the bottom of the halter, and you're ready to teach him how to lead.

Haltering may not be quite so easy with all llamas. A female llama we purchased as an adult led us quite a chase every time we caught her. Fortunately for us, Bobra Goldsmith put on a training clinic for llama owners at our ranch, and she worked with this llama. Bobra's patience was greater than the llama's fear, but it took her over an hour to halter the llama. It would not have taken so long if we had had a catch-pen or restraining chute in the pasture.

Llama halters are available from several mail-order suppliers, and you can often buy them at llama conferences. Kelly even found them for sale recently at our local feed store. A halter should fit snugly enough that it doesn't slop around on the animal's head, but it shouldn't be so tight that it's uncomfortable. When llamas chew their cud, they use a side-to-side movement which the halter must be loose enough to accommodate. It should be taken off the llama when you are not working with him. Some people do leave them on, but llamas have been injured by getting their halters caught. The results in some cases have been death.

Because llamas are a little head-sensitive, they quickly figure out that if they stay close to you, with a loose lead, they won't have to feel any unpleasant pressure on the lead line. Tying a knot or two in the lead rope will make it easier for you to hold the rope. We have taught the llamas to walk behind us, rather than next to us, by tucking the lead rope under an arm.

When you first start walking, the llama may buck or sit down if he doesn't like what you are doing. If he bucks, just hold on tight (those knots in the rope help here, and gloves protect against rope burn) and he'll stop pretty soon.   If he sits down, run at him, yelling "UP! UP!"

Let your first walking sessions be easy, and your llama will develop confidence in you.   Chances are he'll be enjoying his outings, looking around and munching on this and that.   Gradually you can introduce challenges.   We sometimes walk a llama or two down to the mailbox, along the edge of the paved road.   At first they became agitated by cars, but now only the occasional logging truck will surprise them.   I find that loud noises disturb

Llamas are sometimes trained to pull carts. This charming young pair were trained by Lynn Hyder, and are being driven by Judie Palmer.

llamas very little. If there are creeks to be waded or
jumped, cliffs to go up or down (up is easier), give it a
try. Even inexperienced llamas will go many places.
They are incredibly sure-footed.

If a llama doesn't want to go down a steep hillside,
perhaps you can find a less steep place, and from success
there he will conclude that the steep place isn't so bad.
Often if a green llama refuses to do something alone, he
will do it if following behind an experienced one.

I talk to my llamas a lot while walking with them;
they know 'let's go' and that 'okay' means now they may
browse for a while. They have me trained too: they
express 'let's go' and 'hurry up' eloquently through body
language. They're especially fond of 'hurry up' when
we're almost back home.

Combing your llamas gets them used to handling, or
you may simply touch them. Beginning with your hand at
the withers or on the back of the neck, gradually and
with firm pressure move your hand along the animal's
back and up its neck. When you work on the legs, be
alert to possible kicking; some llamas are more ticklish
than others. It will take you several sessions to get the
llama used to some touching; to reach the point where
you can touch a llama absolutely anywhere could be quite
time-consuming. Only one of ours is to that point, and
that is due to the work of his previous owner. The
benefits of handling them include easier wool collection,
more tractability if they should be injured or need you to
handle them for any reason, and a greater friendship
between human and animal.

PACKING

Because adult female llamas are pregnant most of the
time, they are not used for packing. Both intact males
and geldings make good packers. I was surprised at how
easily they learn to carry packs, but then their ancestors
have been doing it for thousands of years. The first time
something is put on his back, a very tame llama may
briefly turn into a bucking bronco, but the show won't
last long. Bobra Goldsmith comments that once a llama
gets over that first surprise, he seems to settle into
packing with an attitude of 'oh yes, I was born for this.'

Going on a commercial llama pack trip is an excellent way to get to know llamas, whether you're thinking of buying some or have already taken the plunge. These trips are offered in many parts of the United States, mainly in the West. Trips are typically several days in length, and graded in degrees of difficulty. Average or better health and fitness is usually required. Some are simple enough that young children and people who are unaccustomed to much exertion can take them. Some packers offer trips customized to your interests and abilities. Many people who go on these trips have never gone backpacking before.

On a typical trip--if there is such a thing--you will be with a small group of people, accompanied by several male llamas. The animals will be carrying food, bedding, first aid supplies, your clothes and other odds and ends. You may be carrying a small daypack with your camera and other things you want handy. Llama packers will

Plenty of delicious food is the rule when you pack with llamas. Here, Levi considers a brunch prepared by Rosana and Kelly.

send you a list of what to bring, and weight limits if any. You will hike, part of the time perhaps leading a llama. The pace allows time for enjoying your surroundings, and you'll have plenty of chances to observe the llamas. The meals are likely to be delicious, as the llamas can carry in lots of fresh food that would break a backpacker's back. Pack trips with a naturalist present, all-women trips, and trips into remote areas are but a few of the choices llama packers offer. See the Resource Guide for a list of packers.

Trips lasting for one day, or for part of a day, are offered by a few llama owners. Kelly and I are among the pioneers in this area, and I think it's something more llama owners will take up. We are fortunate in having beautiful land with spectacular views, just twenty minutes from a tourist town; people come to Ashland primarily to

Char Horning and Poco go for a walk at Juniper Ridge Ranch. His baskets are filled with picnic goodies. (Medford Mail Tribune photo by Steve Johnson)

see the plays put on by the Oregon Shakespeare Festival Association. We enjoy introducing people to llamas with walks which usually last two or three hours, including a picnic brunch or lunch, on our ranch. Our llamas enjoy the walks too; if we are taking one male out of a pasture and leaving others behind, all the llamas crowd around the gate trying to join the fun.

If you buy a llama, you might want your first packing experiences with it to be in company. Some of the llama packers offer special rates for llama owners who bring along a llama.

Packing with a llama by yourself requires the usual camping gear plus one or more male llamas, some kind of pack, and a little llama food. The llamas will browse on what's available, and packers supplement with grain, oats, alfalfa pellets, or other easy-to-carry food. Before you start out on a long trip with a llama, he should already be trained in haltering, leading, carrying a pack, and walking on trails. He should have had some conditioning hikes, too.

If you don't already own a llama, you might find a llama owner who will rent you one. This isn't widely done, but it does happen. You may be required to attend (and pay for) a training session. Naturally, the llama owner must be satisfied that you will provide good care for the animal. It's more like borrowing a child than going to Hertz for a car.

There are many llama packs on the market now. See Issue #21 of 3L Llama for detailed descriptions, submitted by the pack makers, of ten packs. They can be divided into two types: soft packs and frame packs. Most of the packs advertised are soft packs, and many packers find them adequate and simpler. The frame packs are particularly useful in carrying unusual loads. Llamas, once trained, can carry between 20% and 30% of their weight.

Newspaper carrying bags, shopping bags, and many other items have been successfully used in llama packing, though not for heavy loads. What's essential, in any packing situation, is to balance the load evenly. For this a scale meant for weighing fish is helpful, lightweight, and easily transported.

Llama packing is not only for pleasure. Llama owners

Llama packing at Juniper Ridge Ranch. Poco is carrying a home-made pack arrangement, consisting of two Chinese baskets and a leather pack saddle. Tumbleweed's pack is a half-filled Bonny Doon one. (Medford Mail Tribune photo by Steve Johnson)

sometimes bring home firewood via llamas. Llamas have carried surveyors' instruments.

They have been used in the U.S. Forest Service in several parts of the country. Jim Hook, now active as a llama trainer, was a trail maintenance crew foreman for the Forest Service when he first experimented with using a llama to assist with the workload. Burrito was loaned for the summer by Stan Ebel, a llama rancher in Colorado. Jim and his crew found Burrito to be a great asset, regularly carrying sixty pounds of equipment and supplies, sometimes carrying up to eighty pounds. Burrito went through very rough country, often steep and with no trails. He jumped logs and climbed through rocks, sometimes complaining with a whine but always carrying on. Jim noted, "Sometimes when we come to a good view, he will balk. Then he will take a good look all around and continue after about a minute."

He found Burrito to be both intelligent and hardy. He was calmer than a horse or a mule would have been, and more than one potentially tense situation arose where Burrito's temperament was much appreciated. Jim concluded that llamas have real value as packers for trail maintenance crews and others in rugged backcountry situations.

TRANSPORT

Since llamas are smaller than horses and mules, they will fit in smaller vehicles. Our small male Poco is an extreme example: we take him to town in the back of our small Subaru station wagon. Llamas are more commonly transported in pickup trucks, vans, and trailers--horse trailers or smaller ones. They should not be able to jump out of the vehicle, so a pickup must have a cover. It is not enough that the llamas be tied in an open pickup or in one with just a rack. The llama can still jump out and be dragged by the rope; it has happened. Some people tie their llamas, others don't. I am not inclined to tie, after hearing about a llama who strangled to death, tied down in the back of a horse trailer. I don't mean to make this sound like a catalog of horrors; llamas actually transport quite easily. They need headroom, at least enough so they can sit comfortably. Given room to stand up, some llamas will stand for much of a trip. Others will sit.

Bobra Goldsmith starts teaching a llama to load by getting it to jump over a large log. This generally is achieved with just a little coaxing and pulling, and then it's on to the back of her trailer. She puts a board from the bumper to the ground, angled outward so the llama will be forced to stand back enough to jump in rather than to stand against the edge of the vehicle and stop. An old rug (one with a rubber base or otherwise not inclined to skid) is on the floor of the vehicle. Bobra is in the trailer or van, giving a command and pulling. Soon the llama is in the trailer with her. If he resists, she has a handy little block and tackle arrangement which gives her the strength advantage. Usually by the third time the llama is loaded, he has the idea. After that, he will jump in willingly.

Llamas like to use established dung-piles, so on long trips Bobra carries a coffee can with some llama droppings in it. Stopping at a roadside rest area, she sprinkles a few on the ground in an appropriate spot, and the llamas will go there. On one trip of over 4000 miles, the two llamas travelling in the van never used it as a bathroom. Bobra comments, "Travelling cross-country with a well-trained pack llama—or two—is hardly any more trouble than travelling with the family dog."

There is always more to be said about training, packing, and transport. And people are saying it: Bobra is writing a book on training, and the resource guide lists more on these fascinating areas. Don't be surprised if you find a llama reading over your shoulder.

Llamas are good travelers, though few are small enough to travel as Poco does, in the back of our little Subaru station wagon. (Medford Mail Tribune photo by Steve Johnson)

15
Wool

A llama's wool contributes much to its beauty. I love to watch a herd of llamas, observing the nuances of the many hues of wool. The colors range from pure white to appaloosa (which combs out mostly white or beige, with little dark bits here and there) through all shades of brown--golden, reddish, deep and dark--to the rarer gray and black. Black llamas may comb out a dark reddish brown-black or a gray. The white wool, especially, may be dyed.

In South America, llama wool is used for relatively coarse, everyday items such as blankets, bags, and ropes. A friend of mine who lived in Peru said that when the Indians wanted to make something, a pair of socks, for example, they would shear off the amount of wool needed. Alpaca is plentiful in South America, and it is used for the finer items. Here in North America, handweavers and llama owners love llama wool for all sorts of uses.

Llamas vary in the softness, quantity, and length of their wool. Each animal has a genetic predisposition to produce a certain amount of wool, but environmental factors also do enter in. For example, in a study done in La Raya, Peru, adult females produced less than adult males, and this was attributed to the fact that the females were either pregnant or nursing. Another environmental factor is climate; transport a llama from a warm climate to a cold one, and you will see a considerable difference in the wool. The texture and length won't change, but the coat will become thicker.

The llama's coat consists of guard hairs and the softer underwool. The rather stiff guard hairs have the function

In South America, spinning is often done with a very simple hand spindle rather than with a spinning wheel. Wool spinners in Tarija, Bolivia, make a social occasion of it (above). An Indian woman (below), also in Bolivia, weaves a red and yellow blanket of dyed llama wool. (Both photos by Wilhelmine Afra Chance)

of wicking rain or snow away from the surface of the llama's body, while the underwool keeps the animal warm. Llamas vary in the amount of guard hair in their wool; it's usually around twenty per cent, though in some animals it is virtually absent. The contrast in stiffness between guard hairs and undercoat on our Levi's combed-out wool was striking. While I'm chatting with friends, I just pull out the stiff guard hairs. It's easy with his wool, because his guard hairs are darker in color than his soft wool. Whether or not guard hairs should be removed depends on the use to which the wool will be put. For rugs or wall hangings it wouldn't matter, but for a scarf it would.

Llama wool can be softer than sheep's wool, and as soft as alpaca. Because the softness of llama wool varies, much of it is coarser than alpaca. And the alpacas have little or no guard hair. Llama wool has less elasticity than sheep's wool, and sometimes spinners overcome this by mixing in a percentage of sheep's wool when spinning. As little as ten per cent sheep's wool will make a difference, though the actual percentage will vary from one spinner to another and will depend on the product intended. Another method is to spin two-ply all-llama yarn if the yarn will be used for knitting. If neither of these methods is followed, you may end up with a baggy garment. When a handspinner friend of mine, Barbara Hull, offered to knit me a cap from some of my llama wool, I didn't know to tell her that it would be low in elasticity. Consequently my cap ended up capacious, but it does stay on.

REMOVING THE WOOL

Cleaning

The first job is removing the wool. You begin by cleaning the animal, or at least the area where you will be working. Bobra Goldsmith pioneered the use of electric leaf blowers for cleaning dust and dirt off llamas. Mine has a nozzle coming to a rather small point, so I can focus very specifically on a region I'm about to comb. The leaf blower is noisy but doesn't bother the animals after the first few times. Some seem to like the blowing process, leaning into the current of air coming toward them at supposedly a hundred miles an hour. It is astonishing how much dust comes off the llamas, but then they do love to roll in the dirt.

The llamas will still have some debris, how much and what depending on your pasturing situation. Larger bits can be picked out by hand. The smaller stuff is a nuisance, and contributes to the time needed for working with wool. Some you can remove when combing, the rest later.

Combing

Combing and shearing are your choices for removing the wool. Combing yields a softer wool, as relatively few of the guard hairs will comb out and the ends will not have a blunt cut from shears. For these reasons, handspinners prefer combed wool over that produced by shearing. Wherever your llama's wool is longer than about three inches, you can comb; this will vary from one animal to another. Usually the wool along the back of the neck and the topline of the back will be useless. It may be sunburnt, and especially on the back, it is likely to be dirtier. When combing, first you try to comb out any exceptionally dirty parts of the area where you're working, then throw that wool out and comb the cleaned area for wool to keep. I comb my llamas only when their wool is dry.

Since llamas are not inherently fond of being touched, they may move around when you are trying to comb them. Short sessions of about half an hour, or even less, are good at first. I usually tie the animal up next to a wall or fence, or in a stall. Sooner or later, most llamas accept the process.

Beula Williams timed herself while combing; she obtained five ounces of wool in forty minutes. I am usually slower. But combing has the advantage of training the llama at the same time. Whatever else you're doing with your llamas, this training will pay off.

People use a wide variety of implements for combing.

Fine-toothed dog combs, pet rakes, carding brushes, horse's curry combs, and plastic styling combs for people are all used. Bobra keeps a cardboard box from a liquor store, complete with the partitions for the bottles, in her combing area. As time allows for combing, she stuffs the different colored wools into the sections. Beula keeps track of wool animal by animal, and notes the llama's name on the plastic bags in which she sells the wool. Then if someone is making a garment and comes up a little short, Beula can send them more from Bubbles. This is more likely to yield a perfect match than if the purchaser just asked for more brown.

Shearing

Shearing is faster than combing, and more wool comes off. Llama owners use a variety of methods for restraining their animals during shearing. Those with a small herd may train the animals to accept the shearing, but more commonly the animal is restrained by a helper holding it down, by ropes, or by being placed in a restraining chute. (Tranquilizers are used by some breeders, but Rompun, the tranquilizer most commonly used, depresses the central nervous system, and llamas have died while under it. I doubt that the benefit of the wool is worth the attendant risk of death to the animal.) Some llama owners use electric shears, but they can be dangerous; hand shearing blades seem to be more widely used. Many llama owners leave the wool on the neck, if it is too short to be useful. They also leave the tail alone, and they may leave a strip down the center of the back. To prevent sunburn, llamas should not be shorn closer to the skin than about two inches,

One method of shearing Beula Williams calls 'hand picking.' She uses an ordinary sharp pair of scissors to clip the wool off. This can be done in a low-key way, much as one would comb a llama, and it isn't necessary to do the whole animal at once.

Shearing is done in the late spring or early summer, after the danger of cold weather is past but early enough that the llamas have time to grow out their wool by the next cold season. Shearing on a windy day isn't recommended, as the wool will blow around. Combing may be extended later into the summer if the weeds in your pasture don't become a problem.

A shorn llama is an odd sight. Your darling fluff-ball has been turned into skin and bones. Llama owners whose herds are much in the public eye often choose not to shear because the animals are so much less attractive. Other llamas may also find a shorn llama to be a strange sight, and they may ostracize it: good reason to shear more than one at a time. It takes two years for the full coat to grow in after shearing.

USING THE WOOL

The wool yield per animal each year will range from a few ounces for sporadic combing, up to as much as eight pounds off an exceptionally woolly beast. The average is probably in the one to four pound range. Llamas shed some every year, but more heavily every other year, so shearing is often biennial. Combing will always yield less than shearing. Because llamas do not produce lanolin or other oils, llama wool will go much further than an equivalent weight of sheep's wool. Beula Williams measured a pound of llama wool that she had spun single-ply and fine: it was 1406 yards.

The amount of wool you would need for a sweater would, of course, depend upon what kind of sweater you had in mind. I have a South American alpaca sweater, a long-sleeved pullover, which weighs one pound. You would need somewhat more to allow for wastage in spinning, possible dirt in the wool, and the like. But if you mixed it with sheep's wool, that would reduce your need for llama wool.

You can sell the llama wool as is, dirty or clean. You can clean it up, a little or a lot, before selling. If there is a handweavers' guild in your area, just let the word get around and you'll probably sell as much as you want. As a specialty wool, it commands a high price; at this writing, clean wool goes for somewhere around $2 per ounce, depending on its quality.

If you have never spun anything, you may wish to

*A Bolivian woman spins llama wool with a drop spindle.
(Wilhelmine Afra Chance)*

learn. There are many good books available on spinning and weaving, and in many regions you can find a class to take or a person to teach you. Or you might find a spinner in your area who would spin your llama wool for you, in exchange for a portion of it. Llama wool is not customarily washed before spinning, since there is no grease to remove. If you are learning to spin, Beula Williams recommends starting out with a mixture of llama and sheep's wool, and then advancing to llama only; the mixture is easier to handle for both cleaning and spinning. Wash your yarn with a mild detergent.

Serena Linde, a llama owner who teaches spinning, introduces beginning students to the spinning process by having them put a handful of combed fleece on their legs. They draw one hand, palm down, across the wool so that it begins to twist. Holding the twisted fleece stationary, they then use the other hand to draw out the fiber. By doing this, the elemental rhythm of twist and draw out, twist and draw out, becomes clear. She starts them out with sheep's wool. "On a wheel, it's hard until you get the hang of it," Serena says. "There's more motion going on."

Another spinner, Barbara Hull, gave me a spinning lesson on her wheel. "I began on a cute old spinning wheel," Barbara told me, "and it took me a very long time to learn. Now with this Louet, spinning is much easier. I like the size of the hole that the yarn goes through."

Working with two hands and the foot-pedal was like a three-way head-patting and belly-rub, but I felt enough of the rhythm of spinning to be enticed.

Llama wool is used for knitting, crocheting, and weaving. Knit caps and scarves are popular. Lovely and elaborate garments may be woven. A llama-wool sweater is said to be warmer than an equivalent sheep's wool sweater. Coarser wool may be used successfully in rugs and wall hangings.

If you have some llama wool and wish to try something different, consider Australian locker hooking. The yarn needn't be spun for this process. There's a book in the Resource Guide on the method, suitable for rugs and garments.

Many llama owners do little or nothing with llama

wool. But if you're so inclined, a fascinating hobby or
cottage industry comes built-in with every llama.

*Olga Oliver made this pillow with the technique of Australian
locker hooking.*

16

The Business End

In the past decade the price of a pair of weanling llamas has increased from around $1500 to $8000 or more. What happened? A new market was created as llamas became more appreciated as packers, providers of wool, and pets. It seems unlikely that the potential market has come anywhere near being saturated; the number of llamas in this country is very small compared to the numbers of horses, dogs, or other domestic animals.

Llama prices have risen so much; what are the chances of their going down again? Most llama breeders don't think they will, because the interest in llamas is so great. Some breeders have waiting lists now that will take them years to fulfill. Without being able to foresee national and international economic conditions, I'm not going to predict llama prices. Because llamas are intrinsically useful, I think they would have real value under any conditions. Whatever happens, the better animals are just about always a better investment, but remember that there's no real agreement as to what constitutes a better animal. I am by no means a financial wizard, and anything I say about llamas and money could turn out to be wrong, or not to apply to your particular situation for some reason. If you want to get into llamas, do talk with a number of breeders and with any financial advisors you use.

Who buys llamas? First-time purchasers are often people who have been around the animals a little bit, perhaps taken a pack trip, or just visited some llama ranches. I'm always running into people who have thought about buying a llama someday. Some of those

Some publicity is good for business. Here, Poco and Rosana take part in the fourth of July parade in Ashland. (Michael Barth)

people will. Some buy them as a good investment and for tax benefits. Many sales, especially of females, are between breeders.

BREEDING

Llama breeding is an exciting and enjoyable business. I find the birth of a baby llama inherently more satisfying than the rise of the stock market. But breeding is as uncertain as the stock market, maybe even more so. How many male babies and how many female babies will your herd produce this year? Will the babies be healthy? I've heard estimates on the percentage who are born healthy and continue to thrive, ranging from close to 100% down to 80%. Those are overall percentages; in a small herd the occasional mishap can be quite disheartening. Hard facts on survival rates are yet to come.

When we were thinking about buying llamas, I heard a cheerful analysis which went something like this: you buy juvenile females, breed them at about two years of age, have first babies at three, and from then until they die of old age you average a fifty per cent return per year on your original investment--or better, if prices rise significantly. The assumptions implicit in this theory are optimistic: near 100% live annual birth rate, no mishaps, and low overhead for feeding and shelter. It could work out this way, and probably has for some people. But don't count on it.

In doing our own planning, we spent a lot of time with an electronic spreadsheet on my computer. We began with a rather glum set of assumptions: with level prices, a high rate of infant mortality, and more males than females born at first, the return on our investment still looked quite good after the first few years. Assuming modest price increases, about 10% infant mortality, and a 50-50 distribution of sexes, the investment looked better. (With a large sample, the distribution of the sexes will average out near 50-50, but with a small sample it can vary a lot. I've heard of people having nine male babies born in a row, for example.) With near 100% live annual birth rate and no mishaps, things looked very nice indeed. If you have access to a computer and an electronic spreadsheet, it's fascinating and instructive to explore possible scenarios. It will be fun in a few years to pull out our estimates and compare them with what has happened.

What start-up costs are involved? You need the animals, land--your own or rented--to keep them on, fencing, some sheds or shelters, a water source, feeding facilities, a place to store feed, and a way to transport the animals. There will be vet fees. If you attend conferences, there will be those costs. You'll need miscellaneous supplies. If you wish, two main types of insurance are available: named perils covers accidents and theft, and full mortality also includes death from disease.

Start-up capital comes from various places. Many breeders start from their own pockets. Family and other partnerships exist. Bank loans for the llamas themselves are quite rare, but I know of several llama breeders (ourselves included) who put second mortgages on their homes to buy more llamas.

There are many tax implications to raising llamas, and I strongly recommend that you consult with a CPA, preferably one familiar with agricultural taxes. If you go into breeding, you're a farmer, with a new income tax schedule to fill out; the IRS puts out a free booklet for farmers. If you've never been self-employed before, you may be pleasantly surprised at the number of expenses that are tax deductions. Some llama breeders have expressed the view that you need a specific number of llamas to be eligible for tax benefits, but I have heard at least two CPAs refute this belief. You do have to have an intention to earn money, though. Two geldings kept as pets would not be likely to qualify you as a farmer. Our land is subject to lower property taxes because it's being used for agriculture. There are sometimes programs about tax implications of llama raising at the conferences. As with any business, it pays to keep good records and receipts. (That shoebox again.)

What can you expect to earn? A rough rule of thumb a few years ago was that you needed twenty breeding females to consider making your living with llamas alone. Now, with prices up, the number is certainly smaller. If you start small, you may build up your herd by keeping some or all female babies. This practice can extend the time before you see a significant income. Clearly, breeding llamas is not a get-rich-quick scheme. Many llama breeders see little or no profit for the first few years.

The Question of Importation

In 1983, Chile was certified free of foot-and-mouth disease, and for the first time in close to half a century, llamas were imported into this country from South America. Both llamas and alpacas were brought in, as well as some llama-alpaca crosses. There was concern among llama breeders about how importation might affect the market here, as well as pleasure at the opportunity to expand our gene pool. Then in mid-1984, foot-and-mouth disease was found in one region in Chile, and importation was discontinued, at least temporarily. Every llama breeder has a different opinion as to how the importation, if or when resumed, will affect the market. Because alpacas offer a better profit, the importers may focus on them. The llamas who came in were sold at prices in line with animals already in this country, as the importers had substantial costs of paperwork, transportation, quarantines in both Chile and the United States, and so forth. The periodicals and organizations in the Resource Guide can keep you up to date on developments; it's a topic of great interest and some controversy in the industry.

OTHER ACTIVITIES

Packing is another major llama business. There are packing outfits around the country, mostly in the western states, offering a variety of trips. Packers may offer scheduled trips open to the general public, special-interest trips (for example, one for photographers), or trips by special arrangement to groups. Many packers are also breeders, and people who have taken their pack trips are often among their customers for llamas.

There are a variety of other llama-related business possibilities. Wool can be sold just as it comes off the animal, clean or dirty, or it may be spun and used to create clothing, wall hangings, rugs, and other items. Beula Williams, herself a handspinner, expects the cottage industries related to llama wool to increase in many interesting ways, as has happened around packing.

Not everyone has the time or temperament to train llamas, and those who do have a salable service. Some trainers buy male llamas, train them to be far more useful, and re-sell them at a profit. They may train llamas for a fee. At least two offer training clinics, teaching llama owners how to do the training.

Transporting llamas, writing about llamas, making craft

items or importing them from South America, photographing them, mail-order sales of llama-related items, and llama sitting are among the possibilities for earning money that have been explored so far. Many of these ideas are suitable for cottage industry or for large scale enterprise; some no doubt offer more opportunity than others.

For many breeders, the bottom line on llamas has been a nice large bit of black ink. Others haven't yet made a profit from their woolly friends, but expect to in the future. All of us, I believe, look forward to an expanding, vigorous industry, making the pure pleasure of living with llamas available to more and more people.

Dancing Cloud.

17
Resource Guide

Where do you go to find out more about llamas? This chapter lists books, magazines, people, organizations, and other resources. It is necessarily incomplete, because of things I didn't know about, or changes that took place after my press date (September 1984). When writing for information to the people or organizations listed, be sure to send them a self-addressed stamped envelope. Your local public library may have some of the books and periodicals, or be able to borrow them for you from another library. Just as I warned you earlier that there could be errors in Living with Llamas, keep in mind that some of the information in publications listed below could already be out-dated.

ABOUT MY SOURCES

Clearly, a book like this one relies on the work of many other people. My primary written sources were Llama Newsletter, Llama World, Speechless Brothers, and 3L Llama. These works have been essential to my learning process about llamas. Everything in print about llamas that I used as a reference is listed in the next sections, and they are all well worth reading.

The annual ILA conferences have been a major source of information for me. Among others, I have drawn on the presentations of the following speakers, listed in chronological order: in 1982, Dr. William Franklin, "Lama Language: Modes of Communication in South American Camelids"; Sheron Herriges, "Care of Sick and Premature

Babies"; Kay Patterson and Bill McCracken, "Investment Round Table"; and Beula Williams, "Wool." In 1983, Dr. Clarissa Sheldon, "Basic Genetic Principles for Llama Breeders"; Dr. LaRue Johnson, "Llama Nutrition and Feeding"; Kay Patterson, "Birthing and Care of the Newborn Llama"; Andy Tillman, "Breeding Practices--What Works?"; and Sally Taylor, "Pasture Management." In 1984, Dr. George Miller, "Cultural, Mythological, Contemporary Uses of Llamas"; Bob Fenimore, DVM, "Nutrition, Health and Well Being"; a panel on importation of llamas; Murray Fowler, DVM, "Soundness Exam"; and a short paper by Eric Hoffman and Marian Murta, "Preliminary Fleece Assessment Survey for Llama and Alpaca." (Videotapes of many of these presentations are available from John Mallon, listed later in the Resource Guide under "Videotapes.")

Because much of what I learned about llamas came about through conversation with other llama owners, I wasn't always able to reconstruct my sources. If I have left anyone off this list, it is unintentional.

BOOKS ABOUT LLAMAS

Faiks, Jan, Jim Faiks, and Phyllis Tozier. Llama Training: Who's in Charge? Anchorage: Faiks Llama Farm, 1982. (Order from Jim Faiks, 4101 Arctic Blvd, Suite 203, Anchorage, AK 99503.) This manual begins with a statement of philosophy, encouraging us to be persistent, consistent, and enthusiastic in our training. Basic topics covered include halter-breaking, accustoming the llama to being handled, leading, problem animals, dominance, packing, loading into vehicles, and lying down. There are also detailed instructions for rein training, driving, and riding. The writing is clear, and the instructions are enhanced by many photographs. I find myself in disagreement on timing: I think that often llamas learn even more quickly than this book would lead you to expect. But when they don't, or you're trying to undo your own or somebody else's past mistakes, the thorough and patient approach of Llama Training: Who's in Charge? puts you in charge. A revised edition is planned for spring 1985.

Ruck, Ruth. <u>Along Came A Llama</u>. London and Boston: Faber and Faber, 1978. Now out of print. This is a very readable, personal account of how a farm family in Wales came to own a llama, and what happened once they had her. As a child, Ruth Ruck had wanted a llama, and as she says, "it is strange how dreams often come true in the end." She knew virtually nothing about llamas at first, and they learned--sometimes the hard way--as they went along. They were charmed and delighted by Nusta, and she became very much a member of the family, complete with her own box of magazines and newspapers to eat in the living room.

Posey and three-day-old Dancing Cloud.

Tillman, Andy. Speechless Brothers: the History and Care of Llamas. Seattle: Early Winters Press, 1981. This invaluable guide to llama care goes into a lot of detail. The book opens with a history and description of llamas. Other chapters cover packing with llamas; training them; their wool; the language of their ears, tails, and sounds; fencing and shelter; feed; and preventative medicine. Drawings, numerous black and white photographs, a glossary, and an index are included. Tillman knows his topic extremely well: he has been raising llamas since 1975, was a co-founder and president of the International Llama Association, and has studied llamas with an AID program in Peru. Much of the material in Speechless Brothers was not previously available in North America; the book helps to bridge the gap between the often scholarly research done in South America and the llama fancier on this continent.

The first edition is now out of print. Andy Tillman is revising and expanding Speechless Brothers; for ordering information, write to Llama World, at the address below. Highly recommended.

PERIODICALS ABOUT LLAMAS

Llama Newsletter was published from 1978 to 1981, when it was replaced by Llama World. Edited and often written by Andy Tillman, the back issues are available in limited quantity. For ordering information, write to Llama World.

Llama World, P O Box 9293, Seattle, WA, 98119. Editor, Susan Torrey; publisher, Andy Tillman. Write for subscription information. This periodical bears the subtitle "The Magazine of Llama Husbandry and Health," and it runs long and detailed articles, often scholarly, on topics such as color coat inheritance in the llama, the structure and function of the llama stomach, and the use of llamas as pack animals in South America today. Questions and answers, feature articles, and ads are included. Four back copies are available, at $6.25 each; beginning in 1985, it is planned an annual. Highly recommended.

3L Llama, P. O. Box 325, Herald, CA 95638. Published and edited by Bob and Cheryl Dal Porto. Bimonthly (with monthly classified ads), $20 per year. ($25 Canadian per year.) Back copies available. Subtitled "A news and information magazine about llamas and their related uses." Begun in 1979 by Francie Greth and Guy Peto, the 3L Llama has steadily increased in size and scope. It is now a major source of information and communication for the llama community. Articles range over all sorts of llama-related topics; each issue also includes a write-up of a llama ranch, questions and answers, letters, book reviews, and ads. For people thinking about buying llamas, the 3L is an extremely useful way to gain an overview of what's happening with llamas in the U.S. Many llama owners I know sit down and read it the minute it arrives. Highly recommended.

ARTICLES AND PAMPHLETS

Coppinger, Lorna and Raymond. "Livestock-Guarding Dogs that Wear Sheep's Clothing," Smithsonian, April 1982, pp. 64-73. By the people pioneering in this field, the article is about using traditional livestock-guard dogs to protect sheep and other livestock from coyotes and wild dogs. Doesn't mention llamas. (For more information on this topic, write Lorna Coppinger, New England Livestock Guard Dog Project, 731 West St., Amherst, MA 01002.)

Franklin, William L. "Biology, Ecology, and Relationship to Man of the South American Camelids." If you are interested in scholarly research on llamas, alpacas, vicunas, and guanacos, this easily understood technical article includes a bibliography of sources in at least four languages. 124 Science II, Iowa State University, Ames IA 50011.

Franklin, William L. "The High, Wild World of the Vicuna." National Geographic, January 1973, pp. 77-91.

Franklin, William L. "Lama Language," Llama World, Vol. I, No. 2, Summer 1982, pp. 6-11. An introduction to body language, vocalizations, scent communication, and gait.

Franklin, William L. "Living with Guanacos," National Geographic, July 1981, pp. 63-75.

Franklin, William L. "Llama Facts for New Owners," International Llama Association Educational Brochure #3, 1984. Available from International Llama Association. Succinct and fact-filled introduction to llamas.

Garson, Barbara. "Tripping with Llamas," Geo, May 1984, pp. 90-99. The writer's experiences on a trip with Oregon Llamas.

Herriges, Sheron. "Caring for Newborn Llamas," Llama Newsletter, No. 7, pp. 1-3. Also covers birth. A slighty different version appeared in 3L Llama, No. 9, March 1981.

Hook, Jim. "The Llama as a Pack Animal," U.S. Department of Agriculture, Forest Service--Arapaho and Roosevelt NF, December 1980.

Kerstetter, Howard L. "A Few Facts We Know About Llamas," 3L Llama, No. 19, Fall 1983, pp 35-36, 41. About reproduction.

"Llama Packs," 3L Llama, No. 21, Spring 1984, pp. 31-38. Descriptions of ten llama different llama packs you can buy, based on information submitted by the manufacturers. This is neither a complete list nor a Consumers' Report type of evaluation, but still a good place to get an idea of what's available.

Patterson, Kay. "Dystocia," Llama World, Vol. I, No. 1, Spring 1982, pp. 4-7. Very useful article, about both normal and abnormal llama births, by one of the owners of the largest llama herd in the U.S. She's had lots of experience!

Satrom, Gar, and David Stephens. A Fly Control Handbook: IPM for Manure and Compost Ecosystems.

Beneficial Biosystems, 1603 63rd Street, Emeryville, CA 94608. Discusses an alternative to using pesticides in controlling the manure-breeding flies common around livestock. I haven't tried their ideas yet, but I intend to. They sell the fly traps and other items they recommend.

Torrey, Susan. "Llama Wool," Llama Newsletter, No. 2, pp. 1-4. Lots of useful information.

Weisser, Linda. "The Great Pyrenees: A Working Predator Dog," Leaflet written for the Predator Control Committee of the Great Pyrenees Club of America. Available from the author at 4706 Lemon Rd. NE, Olympia, WA 98506.

West, Terry. " 'Suffering We Go:' A Bolivian Llama Caravan," Llama World, Spring 1983, pp.10-15. The author accompanied three highland Bolivian men on a strenuous twenty-two day trip to trade salt for maize.

Williams, Beula. "Observations on Llama Wool," Llama Newsletter, No. 9, pp. 4-5. Very useful.

"Wooly Tidbits," 3L Llama, No. 18, Summer 1983, pp. 7-9, 30. About llama wool, drawing on the knowledge of llama owners and spinners Marian Thormahlen, Pat Warner, and Beula Williams.

OTHER BOOKS

Boone, J. Allen. Kinship with All Life. New York: Harper and Row. This classic consists of anecdotal accounts of two-way telepathy with animals. You may or may not believe it all, but it's fascinating light reading. Much of the book is the story of Boone's communication with Strongheart, a German Shepherd and famous movie star. Later chapters discuss rattlesnakes, skunks, ants, and flies. I enjoyed the book, and so did my dog; it's the only book she ever chewed as a puppy. I haven't given my llamas a chance at it yet.

Clark, Ann Nolan. Secret of the Andes. New York, Viking Press, 1952. Every year the Newberry Award is given to the best children's novel of the year, and this book won it in 1953. It's an enjoyable story with mythic overtones about an Indian boy who is a llama herder learning of his ancient Inca roots. Llamas figure prominently in the story. For older children and adults.

Poynter, Dan. The Self-Publishing Manual: How to write, print, and sell your own book. Santa Barbara, Para Publishing, 1984. Living with Llamas would not have been published without this book.

Rough, Joan Z. Australian Locker Hooking: A New Approach to a Traditional Craft. Glasgow, VA: Fox Hollow Fibres, 1982, $6.95. Order from Fox Hollow Fibres, Rt. 1, Box 161A, Glasgow, VA 24555; add $1.35 for shipping. Step-by-step instruction in a technique which uses loops of unspun wool held in place on rug canvas by a hidden "locking" yarn. Detailed instructions, illustrations, photographs, and one locker hook included in each book.

U.S. Department of Agriculture. Plants Poisonous to Livestock in the Western States. Agriculture Information Bulletin #415. Washington, D.C: U.S. Government Printing Office, 1981, $5.00 postpaid. More than 30 of the principal poisonous plants growing on western ranges are listed and described in this useful booklet, as are the signs of poisoning in livestock. Suggestions are included for the prevention of livestock poisoning by plants. The material is designed to assist owners of sheep, horses and cattle, primarily in open range situations, but llama packers and owners may find it quite useful as well.

It goes into a lot of detail as to how much of a particular plant must be eaten to cause a problem, and under what conditions. For each plant, or group of plants, there is a map showing the distribution in the states west of the Mississippi, one or two clear color photos of the plant, and descriptive text including when and where it grows, how it affects livestock, and ways to reduce livestock losses.

The plants covered are: arrowgrass, bitter rubberweed, chokecherry, copperweed, deathcamas, greasewood, groundsel (threadleaf and riddell), halogeton, hemp dogbane, horsebrush, larkspur, locoweed, lupine, milkvetch, milkweed, nitrate-accumulating plants, oak, pingue (Colorado rubberweed), poison hemlock, ponderosa pine needles, rayless goldenwort, St. Johnswort, selenium-accumulating plants, sneezeweed, spring parsley, tansy ragwort, threadleaf snakeweed (broomweed), western bracken (bracken fern), western false hellebore, and western waterhemlock. Seven other plants, including jimsonsweed and yellow star thistle, are briefly touched upon.

White, Betty and Thomas J. Watson. Betty White's Pet-Love: How Pets Take Care of Us. William Morrow and Company, 1983, $12.95 Animals are good for people. I already knew that, but I still enjoyed Betty White's anecdotes and rundown of research. The human/animal bond is a topic of study; there have even been scientific conferences on it. Llamas are only mentioned once, in a passing reference to a petting zoo.

Lil Bit greets Jan Van Schuyver, while Posey shows her customary shyness mixed with curiosity.

LLAMA ORGANIZATIONS

International Llama Association (ILA) is the larger of the two national llama organizations in the U.S.; most breeders are members. It holds an annual conference open to everyone, and a veterinarians' conference. Other services include an annual directory of members, educational brochures, a quarterly newsletter, and a Hot Line list of informed people willing to respond to questions from ILA members. The Hot Line also includes a list of veterinarians who may be consulted about llamas by any veterinarian. The Camelid Identification System (CIS), established by ILA in 1982, is a computerized database used by owners of llamas and other camelids (alpacas, guanacos, and crosses) for genealogical and other information. Regional chapters are located in California, the Midwest, Northern Rockies, Rocky Mountains, and Washington State. For more information, write ILA, Box 3840, Bozeman, MT 59715.

Llama Association of North America (LANA) offers a computerized tattoo registry system, informative advertising in national publications, annual Expos for llama owners and enthusiasts, a quarterly newsletter, a library of videotapes and publications, and a membership directory. For more information, write LANA, P. O. Box 1174, Sacramento, CA 95806.

The following regional groups are not presently affiliated with either national group:

Northeast Conference of Llama Lovers, c/o Marty McGee, RD 2, Box 167D, Dundee, NY 14837.

Southwestern Llama Association, c/o Terry and Kathy Price, 925 West Culver Street, Phoenix, AZ 85007.

LLAMA PACK TRIPS

There are more llama packers every season, and with a wider geographical spread. I wrote to every llama packer I could find, asking for current information and a brief description of any specialties. Some llama packers were probably too busy to answer, as I wrote in mid-summer. Presence on this list is not an endorsement, and absence from it is no criticism. (I asked for the year that they started business, but I may not have been clear enough that I meant the packing business, so some dates may refer to the llama business in general.) Many of these packers have brochures.

Aspen Mountain Llama Treks, (Denny Krieger), 0365 Red Dog Rd., Carbondale, CO 81623. (303) 963-0261. 1982. "Guided hiking, fishing, climbing in the high Colorado mountains."

Cabin Peak Llamas, (Patricia McCarthy and Gerry Sammon), 4686 Midview Drive, Palo Cedro, CA 96073. (916) 547-3836. 1981.

Cascade Llama and Packing Company, 14955 168th Ave. NE, Woodinville, WA 98072. (206) 487-3612. 1982. "Trips primarily in Alpine Lakes Wilderness. Young families (children) welcomed."

Earth Cousins Llama Ranch (Laurel and Don Osborne), 405 W. Washington St., Suite 27, San Diego, CA 92103. (619) 765-2288. 1983. "Year-round treks, Southern California mountain areas, specializing in survival techniques/classes while hiking and camping."

Frick Llama Journeys, (Terry Frick and Bo Hanson), P O Box 7663, Bend, OR 97708. (503) 389-3738 or (503) 382-6332. 1984. "Lighten your load. . . lift your spirits. . . lead a llama!"

Great Divide Llamas, (Stan Ebel), 7902 N County Rd 27, Loveland CO 80537. (303) 667-7411.

Great Northern Llama Co., (Steve and Sue Rolfing), 1795 Middle Rd., Columbia Falls, MT 59912. (406) 755-9044. 1981. "Custom trips, small groups, fishing, Glacier National Park region."

High Country Llamas, (Steve and Peggy Kramer), 34106 Gap Rd., Golden, CO 80403. (303) 642-7672. 1981. "Wilderness packing."

Home Ranch Llama Trekking, (Peter Nichols), Box 190K, Clark, CO 80428. (303) 879-1780. 1981. "Great fishing, gourmet meals from a crackling campfire—deluxe wilderness pack trips our specialty."

Juniper Ridge Ranch, (Kelly and Rosana Hart), P O Box 777, Ashland, OR 97520. 1984. "Two-hour walks with llamas and a picnic on our ranch.   Wheelchair access."

Lost Coast Llama Caravans, (Nancy Peregrine), 77321 Usal Rd., Whitethorn, CA 95489. No phone. 1982. "Many all-woman trips."

Mama's Llamas, Inc. (Francie Greth and Guy Peto), P O Box 655, El Dorado CA 95623. (916) 622-2566. 1977. "Naturalist-Guide led treks in California and Peru."

Noah Llama Treks, Inc. (Penny Alsop and Judy Fee), 412 Blowing Rock Rd., Boone, NC 28607. (704) 264-0509. 1983. "First llama treks east of the Rockies. All gear provided."

North Star Llamas, (Glenn and Claudia Roberts), S.R.A. Box 6013, Palmer, AK 99645. 1984. "We offer easy day trips enjoying Alaska's abundant scenery."

Oregon Llamas, (Tom and Toni Landis), P O Box 96, Brownsville, OR 97327. (503) 466-5976. 1981. "High quality wilderness outings in Oregon's Cascades."

Rocky Mountain Llama Treks, (Steve Eandi), Sugarloaf Star Route, Boulder, CO 80302. (303) 449-9941. 1980. "Quality wilderness packing for specialized groups or individuals of all ages."

San Juan Llama Company, (Joyce and Dennis Adams), P O Box 5110, Durango, CO 81301. (303) 247-9757. 1984. "Custom pack trips for small groups into high, remote areas."

Sierra Llamas, (Ken and Sharon Hansgen), P O Box 509, Loomis, CA 95650. (916) 652-0702. 1981. "Three-day weekend getaway treks, Tahoe Sierra region, small groups."

Siskiyou Llama Expeditions, (Chant Thomas and Melanie King), P. O. Box 1330, Jacksonville, OR 97530. (503) 899-1696. 1983. "Visit endangered wilderness; custom trips available; small groups; extended or day trips."

Vagabond Llamas, (Terry and Kathleen Price), 925 W Culver, Phoenix, AZ 85007. (602) 253-3302. 1983. "Specialize in families with young children. Trips in Arizona and Colorado."

Wilderness Way Llamas, (Jodi and Don Sleeper), P O Box 449, Espanola, NM 87532. (505) 753-6829. 1982. "Specializing in participation and learning the joys of llama packing."

Willie's Woolies, (Kathy and Randy Williams), P O Box 871814, Wasilla, AK 99687. (907) 376-3643. 1984.

MAIL-ORDER LLAMA SUPPLIES

There are a number of mail-order businesses; here are two of the older ones. To find out about others, check ads in the llama periodicals and booths at conferences.

Llamas & More, 26245 Horsell Road, Bend, OR 97701. Gifts and gear; write for free brochure.

Rocky Mountain Llamas, 5893 Baseline Road, Boulder CO 80303. Llama equipment for grooming, packing, and driving. Write for free catalog.

OTHER

Jones, Susan L., 104 Hickory Mill, Kent, OH 44240.
(216) 678-8174. Susan has a very complete stock file--over
1000 shots--of llama photographs, both black-and-white
and color transparencies.   All aspects of llama behavior,

There is a natural affinity between children and llamas. (Susan L. Jones)

beauty, and fun are covered. Advertising photos available. Many of her photographs have been published in the 3L Llama, and there are several in this book.

Rocky Mountain Laboratories, 2107 Templeton Gap Rd., Colorado Springs, CO 80907. (303) 636-2883. Offer various hormone and other veterinary lab tests; we use the progesterone test which indicates pregnancy.

VIDEOTAPES

Mallon, John, 19526 Rancho Ballena Rd., Ramona CA 92065. John was the official videographer for the 1983 and 1984 International Llama Association conferences. Write for list of tapes for sale.

Warner, Chuck. Pet-A-Llama Ranch, 215 Gossage Way, Petaluma, CA 94952.

WOOL

Creek Water Wool Works, P O Box 716, Salem, OR 97308. Buys and sells llama wool, among other things. Free catalog.

McGee, Marty, Home Wools, RD 2, Box 167D, Dundee, NY 14837. Custom spinning, weaving, and knitting of llama wool; also sales of spinning and wool preparation equipment. Send $1.00 for samples and information.

Warner, Pat, Pet-A-Llama Ranch, 215 Gossage Way, Petaluma, CA 94952. Buys llama wool, based on color and her need at the time. Query her before sending.

Index

COLOPHON

Living with Llamas was written on a Kaypro II computer, and typeset with a Silver Reed 550 printer, using the Modern Proportional Space daisy wheel. Chapter headings (set in Korinna) and photo captions (set in Chelmsford Italic) were done by Todd's Typography, Medford, Oregon. The book was designed by Kelly and Rosana Hart, with help from Michael Bass. Photographs not credited were by Kelly or Rosana Hart. Printing was by Braun-Brumfield, Inc., of Ann Arbor, MI, using 60 pound natural smooth paper, perfect binding, and a 10 pt. CIS cover, film laminated, with black ink and PMS color #167.

Order Form

If the coupon has been clipped, or if you prefer not to use it, just send $10.95 for each copy of <u>Living with Llamas</u> you want. Shipping and handling are included in the price. Make checks out to JUNIPER RIDGE PRESS. You may use a credit card, if you wish; send us the number, whether it's MasterCard or Visa (they are the ones we can accept), the expiration date, and your signature. Please print your name and address LEGIBLY, and send your order to:

Juniper Ridge Press
P.O. Box 777
Ashland, OR 97520

If you want your copies autographed by the author, tell us. You may return any book for a full refund if not satisfied.

— — — — — — — — — — — — — — — — — — — —

TO JUNIPER RIDGE PRESS, P. O. BOX 777,
ASHLAND, OR 97520

Enclosed is $_____ for _____ copies of <u>Living with Llamas</u>, at $10.95 postpaid for each copy.

Check, cash, money order, MasterCard, or Visa welcomed. If credit card: Mastercard ____ Visa ____
Card number _____
Expiration date _____
Your signature is required for credit card orders:

PLEASE PRINT LEGIBLY:
NAME:

ADDRESS:

CITY: STATE: ZIP:

☐ Check here if you want autographed copies.